FOOLISH FAITH

Pushing Past Your Pain to Pursue a Life of Your Dreams

ANASTASIA D. HUNTER

13TH & JOAN

Foolish Faith. Copyright 2021 by Anastasia D. Hunter. All rights reserved. No part of this publication may be reproduced, distributed, or transmitted in any form or by any means, including photocopying, recording, or other electronic or mechanical methods, without the prior written permission of the publisher, except in the case of brief quotations embodied in critical reviews and certain other noncommercial uses permitted by copyright law.

For permission requests, write to the publisher, addressed "Attention: Permissions Coordinator," 205 N. Michigan Avenue, Suite #810, Chicago, IL 60601. 13th & Joan books may be purchased for educational, business or sales promotional use. For information, please email the Sales Department at sales@13thandjoan.com.

Printed in the U. S. A.

First Printing, May 2021.

Library of Congress Cataloging-in-Publication Data has been applied for.

ISBN: 978-1-953156-38-9

To every woman...

...who feels like she made a mistake that threw her so off course nothing would be able to rectify the time lost.

...who feels like if only she made a different turn, a different choice, a different decision, that she wouldn't be where she is in this moment.

...who feels shattered. Your brokenness is welcome here. But don't get too comfortable with it. The way my God is set up, He is turning it around for your good.

CONTENTS

INTRODUCTION 3

HAPPY 16ᵀᴴ BIRTHDAY, STACEY! 7

CHAPTER ONE 11
WATCHING SOMEONE YOU LOVE EVOLVE IS LIKE HEAVEN IN MOTION.
THAT SOMEONE IS YOU.

CHAPTER TWO 29
TRANSPARENCY IS THE MOTHER OF TRANSFORMATION

CHAPTER THREE 45
I ONLY LOST ONE THING I EVER WANTED BACK…MYSELF

CHAPTER FOUR 65
YOU CAN BE THE ONE HE MARRIES AND STILL GET PLAYED

CHAPTER FIVE 91
THE MIRACLE AND THE MISTAKE ARE THE SAME THING

HAPPY 28TH BIRTHDAY, STACEY! 117

CHAPTER SIX 121
   SOMETIMES GOD WILL ANSWER YOUR PRAYER, YET YOUR SITUATION WON'T CHANGE. BUT SOMETHING EVEN BETTER WILL. YOU.

CHAPTER SEVEN 147
   BOUNDARIES; YOUR VALUES IN ACTION

CHAPTER EIGHT 173
   DECIDING WHO YOU ARE MEANS DECIDING WHO YOU WILL NEVER BE AGAIN

CHAPTER NINE 197
   QUEENS ARE NOT BORN; THEY ARE AWAKENED

CHAPTER TEN 225
   WHAT'S THE POINT OF FAITH IF YOU DO NOT BELIEVE GOD CAN PERFORM MIRACLES…FOR YOU?

FINAL THOUGHTS 267

ACKNOWLEDGMENTS 269

While reading, you will see letters I've written referencing myself as Anastasia and as Stacey. Anastasia is who I am today; the empowered woman I evolved into after the storm. Stacey was young. She was naïve. She wanted whatever she set her eyes on and made a way to get it without thinking of the possible consequences. These letters serve as a reminder that I could not have become who I am in this moment without the version I was as a young girl. Every season in my life was necessary.

Foolish Faith is written in both past and present time. I chose to write that way because as I piece together various times in my life, I could feel the depth of my own emotions emerge. It is integrated with thoughts I've written in a diary in those moments and in my own thoughts as I type. Writing this was HARD. It is by far one of the most difficult things I have ever done in my entire life. There are moments while reading where you will witness me encouraging myself to continue despite my own fear. That is typical when you are doing God's work.

Even though I have evolved from those moments, I still want to connect to the woman who may be currently experiencing her own storm. We are all one and the same. At the risk of exposing my own skeletons, I bow down to you, to lift you up in knowing you aren't alone. I want you to know that you can go through it, still heal, and level back up, too. This will live up to its genre. It is not condescending nor is it unrelatable. I am only as strong as the woman reading this.

At the end of each chapter, you will see a QR code. Here is a two minute takeaway of me summarizing what I have learned about myself, or the situation I was facing at that moment. To view the video, simply open the camera application on your phone and hold your phone over the QR code. A website address will drop down. Click the link, and it will take you directly to that video.

I sincerely pray you will enjoy reading *Foolish Faith* and that my story will cause you to see the beauty in your own.

Hey Queen...YES YOU!!

Do you ever come across old pictures of yourself and get blown away by how much you've evolved? When I look at an old photo, it brings me back to the exact place and time where I can literally feel the depth of emotions that I was experiencing in that moment. There are some photos where I don't recognize that version of myself at all. The stress took such a toll, that I literally didn't look the same. I reflect and remember that there was once a time where I wasn't sure how long those feelings of discomfort would last. I would vow to myself to never be in that same place again. I thank God that He changed me in such a way to ensure that it *didn't* happen again.

I have come to realize that every single woman I look up to had a turning point in her life where she made a clear, specific, definite decision that she was not going to live her life going forward as she once knew. No woman makes this choice at the same age, but the turning point typically happens when she encounters a painful situation that causes her to question everything she once thought about herself. For me, that experience happened at age 28. I thought I knew who I was until life showed me different. I thought

I was in control until it spiraled so quickly that I couldn't keep up. Life showed me that I knew nothing at all. This journey of self-discovery didn't happen overnight. It began with a marriage, and then shortly thereafter, a divorce. I knew I'd settled and that my marriage would never be the happily-ever-after that I'd envisioned. Some women are able to pivot quickly but for me, I had to hit rock bottom. I couldn't pick myself up as swiftly as I could in previous relationships or other circumstances.

I have grown on this journey, and I know it was necessary for this experience to happen in the way that it did in order for me to make the crucial changes I needed to make in my life. These changes required me to come face-to-face with my fears, guilt, and insecurities. The things I once buried had developed roots and those roots came springing forth and out, right to the forefront of my spiraling life. My childhood issues were now adult issues, and I had difficulty navigating the trauma from my past, my current pain, and trying to rebuild and create a new life for myself simultaneously. I now had to map out a new me!

> **God often uses our deepest pain as the launching pad of our greatest calling.**

God often uses our deepest pain as the launching pad of our greatest calling.

I knew I would never be the same again.

I saw glimpses of the woman I could become and I made a promise to jump every hurdle and push through every trial to become her. More often than not, when you leave a negative situation, uncertainty will show up. The feelings of uncertainty can feel so isolating that it might even make you consider going back. Even when you attempt to return, God stops you in your tracks, and confines you while He permeates every broken piece of your being.

I want you to entertain the idea that your biggest insecurity may also become your biggest strength. It's something about knowing that God is in control that just makes you move differently. It makes you feel empowered, unshakable, and extremely confident. Not confident in your own ability, but in the ability of the ONE who is within you, ahead of you, and behind you. God will stop everything you've been trying to do on your own and then release it all at once so you know that it's Him. Do not be discouraged on your journey. Everything God allows has a distinct purpose.

Let this year be the year that you become more of who you really are. Not the version of yourself that makes you comfortable. And definitely not the version of yourself that makes others comfortable. But the version of yourself that you imagine yourself to be when you are free.

"God is within her, she will not fall."
— Psalms 46:5 New International Version

Happy 16th Birthday, Stacey!

I've been trying to find the words to write this letter for days. It took me some time to actually get the words on paper, as I knew I would cry through the entire thing because I feel everything so passionately and so deeply. Yes, you outgrew those hardened, insensitive days.

    I know you're anxiously reading this, so concerned to get to the end to reveal the person you came to be. Take your time, read carefully, and digest intensely. Patience is still a weakness of yours.

    I am not writing this to tell you that things are going to change or that you're going to grow so much because you already know that. The future is unpredictable. If we could gaze into it, we would know to avoid certain situations and relationships, allowing us to smoothly sail through the duration of our short lives. Even though you wish for it, that is not possible.

    If you learn a very important lesson early, you will save yourself so much misery. That lesson is to trust God and even more imperatively, to trust His timing. It's that simple. You have a serious problem with needing to be in control.

You are a perfectionist. You want to have it all figured out. You want to connect every single dot. You want to avoid confrontation, exposure, and struggles at all cost. That's why you feel so much anxiety. It will take you twelve years to learn this lesson. In the end, you will learn that you were never in control.

You will become consumed with appearing that you have it all together to protect your image. You did what many will do at that crossroad—you hid. You hid the parts of you that you deemed were not good enough. You will photoshop your sadness into fake joy so that everyone around you could feel comfortable in your presence.

You will move 2,000 miles away, alone. You are sheltered and inexperienced at life. This experience will show you exactly what you are made of. Living in a new state will be incredibly difficult. It's uncomfortable, expensive, and lonely. It will change your outlook on other people, society, and even yourself. You will be challenged in ways you never knew were possible. You will dive headfirst into situations that you will need to beg God to get you out of. You will forcefully learn who you are at your core because you put yourself in such a vulnerable position.

You will allow others to overdraft you while you invested in them. Your heart will be broken because you served yourself to someone who didn't recognize your worth. Because of this, you will learn the difference between being loved and being valued.

FOOLISH FAITH

You will make temporal things permanent. You're afraid to let go of the people, places, and things that make you the most comfortable. But you learn that greatness never comes from comfort zones.

You will try to dodge the process. You will exhaust yourself into realizing that you need to just get through it. Eventually, you will allow it to teach you so you never have to see it again.

Don't be afraid of the future. Will it be scary? Absolutely. Will you lose your way? Unfortunately, yes. Will it be painful? More than you think...but I can promise you that sometimes it takes losing everything that you thought mattered to realize God is the only thing that matters.

There is a tug on your heart to be great, to live beyond everything you saw and grew accustomed to. Everything you want lies on the other side of your fears. You will find your lane. Once you find it, you will become unstoppable. No one is messing with you in your lane. There is no competition in your lane. No one is you, and that is your power.

You will get discouraged. You will want to break down. You will want to quit. But in order to win, you must defeat yourself.

I love you, baby girl.

Anastasia

CHAPTER ONE

WATCHING SOMEONE YOU LOVE EVOLVE IS LIKE HEAVEN IN MOTION.

THAT SOMEONE IS YOU.

"You need to persevere so that when you have done the will of God, you will receive what He has promised."

— Hebrews 10:36 New International Version

MANY TIMES, WHEN God gives us a vision, we sit on it. We ponder if it was truly a message from God. We debate the "what ifs" to death. We question ourselves when the vision we received and our own desires don't line up with the way we expected God to deliver the message. And ultimately we do nothing with what we've received from God and attempt to move forward with our lives. Yet we still ask for guidance, an increase in our blessings, and insight on how to get to our next level.

Shortly after I left my ex-husband in 2016, God gave me foresight for *Foolish Faith*. I share more about the in-depth details in the upcoming chapters. Just wait; it was tumultuous, to say the least. I kept a diary of what was transpiring at the time for the sole purpose of this book. Truthfully, I promised myself I would never speak of the details of my failed marriage. I was utterly embarrassed and humiliated. I wanted to hide under a rock and forget every single, hideous moment. Many nights I prayed for God to supernaturally rewind the time so I could've done things differently, so that I could have made better choices. I've started and stopped writing so many times. Ultimately, I took a very long hiatus. I hoped that God's direction for me to write would take a left turn and detour to another task He wanted me to complete. I would rather roll down a cliff than develop the courage to write about the most disgraceful moment in my life.

I am writing this very chapter on my 32nd birthday in 2019. I spent the majority of the day crying in frustration because after three years of being single, content, and happily working on me, nothing in my life has drastically changed. I feel stuck and stagnant. I have yet to see the manifestation of almost everything I prayed, hoped, wished, and begged God for. Why aren't things changing? I ask this question on a daily basis. I've been in a season of wilderness for nearly four years, and I don't know how to get out. I felt I've done the work. I've looked in the mirror. I've done the self-reflection. I've recounted every single act in which I've done something or someone wrong. I've been humbled beyond belief. I've taken full accountability for my own actions and how I ended up here. I realize I didn't make smart choices. But many people make questionable choices, and it seems as though God gets them right back on track, right? Why was this not happening in my own life even though I was doing the work?

As I lay in bed, tears flowing down my cheeks soaking my pillow, a warm presence literally surrounded me and took over my body. It was as if someone walked into my bedroom, right past me, and the air shifted. It startled me. The last time I felt this feeling was the very first night I slept in my apartment after I left my marriage. I knew He was there. I felt safe. This experience is beyond words and indescribable unless you've experienced it for yourself. Those of us that have had God save us from ourselves, deliver us, and rewire us into better versions can understand the depth and intensity of emotion I am speaking of. In that moment, I listened.

I immediately thought of this book. I knew what God was saying. It was time to share this story. Like many people, I didn't want to share my story while I was still struggling. I wanted to share it when it was far back in the rearview mirror. You know, out of sight, out of mind. God told me that wanting to wait until life was rosy is not the perspective He wants written. Nothing is more raw than describing struggle while you are still in the struggle, but I have never been more desperate for a supernatural touch from God. I have never been more desperate for a life shift than I was at this very moment. I hear you, Lord. I'll do it.

It took me 32 years to not only realize, but to believe that someone is looking for me. The authentic version of me. Not the prim and polished Stacey, or the determined Stacey that's relentless in her goals today. But the Stacey that cried herself to sleep, or the Stacey that should have lost her mind. The Stacey that left her marriage with nothing but courage to leave. The Stacey that was homeless and couldn't find a new place to live because her credit had gotten so bad no landlord would accept her. Not Stacey's highlight reel. Someone is looking for me, so that they'll have permission to be themselves. Permission to stand confidently in her truth. Someone is looking for that in you, too. It's okay to not be polished all the time. It's okay to admit that we took a few wrong turns. It's okay to be REAL. We are not supposed to be perfect.

The Most Beautiful Things Are Birthed out of Your Discomfort

I am not an author. I haven't been writing because I just feel that I can't. This is beyond me. I am an educated woman, but becoming an author was never on the list of things

I wanted to achieve. This task makes me completely vulnerable and insecure. I don't have an eloquent writing style. My writing does not flow like poetry. I am more of a "straight shooter, straight to the point" kind of gal. When I decided to get serious, I prayed hard, asking God to give me the words to say because this is so beyond my comfort zone. If God did not make my thoughts flow directly to

> **Foolish Faith is me sharing my story in whole truth.**

my fingertips, this would not get done. Each time I sit down to type, I pray to God, asking for His thoughts to become my own. I didn't believe in my own ability. I questioned who would receive my thoughts and if my thoughts were even worthy of being shared. I can speak about this in a small group setting, but what about those who won't get me? Those who won't understand me? I am afraid of that. The fear is that if I share the dark parts of my story, I will be judged. My image will be shattered. *Foolish Faith* is me sharing my story in whole truth. My prayer is that anyone who may read this will feel God's presence and experience a life-changing encounter with Him directly. Regardless of how uncertain I feel in this moment, I will share my scars so that you may heal.

In 2016, I remember being in my apartment with just my dogs literally screaming at myself for the choices I made.

How did I get HERE? How stupid did I have to be to let my life fall apart like this? I've never spoken to myself in such a demeaning, defeating, criticizing tone as I did that year. I thought that season would destroy me. That I made a decision I could never bounce back from. That I would forever be scarred. That I could never make up for lost time. I prayed day and night for every ounce of pain to leave my body. I prayed I could stop feeling like everyone was staring at me. I didn't go out in public much—only for necessities. Whenever I stepped out and someone's eyes met mine for a moment too long, I felt that they were laughing at me.

> **Falling apart is nothing we ever want but becomes everything we've ever needed.**

Falling apart is nothing we ever want but becomes everything we've ever needed. It's the perfect reason to reassess and reinvent ourselves. We all love the idea of "newness." However, the journey to getting a new car, a new house, or a new life is often very difficult. A new version of your life starts with disrupting the current one. The consistency in my life was part of the reason I had gone to such a dark place. It was easy to keep doing what had gotten me there rather than try something new. I could get myself in and out of situations with ease, and I've always made pretty solid decisions. I may have had my back against the wall, yet nothing was too hard for me to figure out—but nothing had been like this. This was a jam I couldn't get out of. Have you ever caught yourself in the fetal position crying out to God? You are completely, utterly helpless. But in this space, God can speak to you. In this position, you are willing to hear the voice of God because, sadly, it is your last resort. You have no other option of manipulating the situation on your own. As much as I prayed for God to snatch me out of that time in my life, I can see clearly now that He delivered me *through* the fire—He didn't deliver me *from* it. God doesn't always take us out of a problem. A lot of times, He stretches our faith by taking us through the problem. Going through that marriage and divorce was a defining moment in my character that humbled me. God knows exactly what it takes to push you into His purpose.

The time between leaving my marriage and this moment on my birthday forced me to evolve beyond belief. Beyond anything I had the mental and emotional capacity to ask for. It may not be the material manifestation of what I wanted, but there is something about waiting...and waiting on God. The intense pressure you feel, but also the laser sharp focus you develop. Going through hard times will change how you communicate with God. Your anxiety unfolds into maturity. The purpose of pain is to move us into action to unlock new levels of faith. Replacing "God, why are you letting this happen to me?" with "God, what are you trying to teach me?" was the shift I needed to finally allow the change I was begging for to find me. What you see may not always reflect what God is doing, and what you feel may keep you from believing that God is moving. Our faith causes us to hold on to our belief despite what we feel and see. We can believe He is shifting, moving, healing, removing, adding, and disrupting things because there is a plan greater than the life we settled for.

These years gave me so much compassion toward others. I know how it feels to hurt behind a bright white smile. While you've tricked the world into thinking you have it all together, you're falling apart internally and are forced to come face to face with your poor decision making and your ego. Life is hard, and everyone is simply doing the best they can with what they have. One decision can either change our lives for the better or for worse. So we can never judge a person or a situation, regardless of who put them there.

As the embarrassment faded, I began to post quotes on Facebook promoting self-love. I didn't see inspiration tailored to my own situation, so I needed to create it myself. This led me to feel confident enough to post that I was divorced. Divorced and free, not bitter, because I truly believe God gave me a second chance. I began to receive messages from women—some I knew from school, others I'd never met. They shared their own experiences with traumatic relationships—and some were still in them. I was surprised, yet humbled, that women felt comfortable enough to share the most intimate details of their lives with me. Hearing similar stories from women who were in or have experienced similarities to what I had aided in my decision to talk about it instead of suffering in silence. What I truly wanted was to act as if it never happened. God cannot heal what you hide. We tend to hide our truth behind perfectly contoured faces, fly clothing, lifetime achievements, and refined external behaviors. *Foolish Faith* is to call you out to a place of honesty, to provide hope, reconciliation, and forgiveness to others, but most importantly to yourself. God will never give us an extraordinary blessing in an ordinary place. We must overcome obstacles, climb up steps we cannot see, and walk down paths that aren't paved to get the glory that God has in store for us. Had He not kept me still and allowed me to be as busy as I desired with my life and career, I would have never stopped to tell this story.

I spent nearly four years praying to God and not hearing Him. At the time, I believed He wasn't hearing me! Every part of my faith was challenged. I saved Scriptures to recite

> **We tend to hide our truth behind perfectly contoured faces, fly clothing, lifetime achievements, and refined external behaviors.**

when necessary and would never see them show up in my life. I just knew God was angry with me. I came to the conclusion that I just needed to accept the fact that my life had become what it was, and I needed to be thankful that I made it out of my situation alive. I definitely didn't think I would see myself thriving. The silence of God has nothing to do with abandonment. It has everything to do with stillness. Sometimes, who you become in the process of waiting is more impactful than what you are waiting for. God won't move faster simply because you accuse Him of not moving fast enough. Or when you accuse Him of not being there at all. He moves at the rate of your ability to take in. Many times, it's too soon or simply put, "you're not ready." You can't say you trust God but not His timing. There is beauty in being molded in this season of waiting. He is allowing you to see if in this process, you're seeking Him for what you need or for who He is. God's arrival is always on time and always on point. Nothing that is meant for you will be missed. I hope that you can grasp that He is not being cruel, He is being cautious. He knows the damage of some of your wants. Waiting on God can put even the most spiritual woman's faith to a test, but He is always worth the wait.

> **The silence of God has nothing to do with abandonment. It has everything to do with stillness.**

Problems and crises are often God's chosen tools to develop character in us. When He allows these situations in our lives, it is to build our character so we are equipped for the next level of destiny and greatness He has in store. What you go through is not meant to destroy you, it is meant to develop you. God allows us to experience all that we have so we can help others that are facing or will face our same battle. If we always make the right choices and if our lives were always perfect, we would never truly know how to uplift others. Every experience, every hurt, every tear, every disappointment, has prepared you for your unique journey.

Foolish Faith helped me to realize that the things that "happened" to me were never about me. A lot of my hardship was not just for me and my own growth. God is never selfish like that. It was designed with other women in mind. Transparency is a gift! You go through to help others come through. I know about being bullied, abusive relationships, toxic relationships, soul ties, depression, stress, homelessness, suicidal thoughts, infidelity, loving someone beneath my worth, low self-esteem, being misunderstood, divorce, and so much more. This was not all for me. I endured and passed each test so I can help you! When you are at your lowest, I can tell you how great God is. I live as a reminder that if God did it for me, He can do AT LEAST that much for you! Everything you overcome is meant to help someone else. Your voice should speak victory. Your pain has purpose. If it weren't for my pain, I would not be able to connect with you.

If you don't take the time to allow God to build you up, He can't pour into you, and you can't pour into others from an empty cup. Some seasons are solely about growing spiritually, and in other seasons, you will be super busy. Whatever season God has you in, trust His plan for your life because He knows exactly where He is leading you. For the first time, I can say that I am thankful for my seasons of being still and growing.

Your Pain Is a Butterfly That Just Wants to Be Free

Until we have been broken, we don't know what it is to be made whole. I promised God if He gave me another chance to win, I would commit to allowing Him to use me for His purposes. Our journeys are very personal. God is aware of our intentions and is aligning our paths to fulfill our purposes. Do not allow anything to get in the way of you walking in your purpose. I am only here because I believed I was worthy of another chance to live my best life. Your pain is a temporary home for transformation. It is not meant to stay with you, become you, nor cage you. It is meant to teach you. It is a masterclass. What do you believe? Do you truly believe that you are deserving of more? A second chance? An opportunity to thrive and not just to merely exist? You can't win at life without first winning in your mind. Everyone has a story. Everyone has a journey. But everyone doesn't take control of their destiny. Please don't let that be you. The enemy is after our expectations. He wants us to accept that what we have and what is right in front of us currently is all we will ever have. He wants us to think that we will never be able to come back from our mistakes. That we took too many left turns for God to get us right again. What God has purposed for your life is too important for you to leave your issues unconfronted.

Reminisce on those days when you were so fearless you believed nothing was impossible. You lived in a childlike element and believed you could be whatever you wanted to be in this world, no matter how foolish or irrational it seemed. I want to resonate with that pure, innocent version of you. By the end of this, I want you to believe that you are still on the right path to becoming the person you always knew you could be. That everything that has happened to you was divinely orchestrated to bring to you this very moment. Taking control of your life will require you to first get control over your mind. I'll be honest, *Foolish Faith* will make you uncomfortable. Nothing will be off limits, so it is imperative that you read with an open mind. Low self-esteem, parental issues, guilt, and authenticity are all topics that we will explore. It won't be easy, but nothing worth having is ever easy. This will be worth it.

Trusting God comes down to first making peace with your path. You can't resent where you are or what you've been through and expect the best. Bitterness and joy cannot coexist. One of the hardest periods in life to go through is your transition from one version of yourself to another. Self-forgiveness is one of the most difficult parts of your healing process.

If you are like me, you have a burning desire to get something out of you, to share with the world or to remain private, confined within the walls of your own home——whether it is written, spoken, or art. That desire is God speaking to you. It will not go away. It will get deeper. It will get louder. God will disrupt your entire life just to speak to you. He will get your attention. You will not be able to move forward into your other goals until you grasp what He is trying to tell you. There is no person in the Bible who God spoke to or gave a task to who could go forth and complete it on their own. It is no different for any of us. Any direction you get from God will require you to ultimately depend on Him to complete it. You will have to pray for guidance and direction every step of the way. God will not require of you what He has not resourced within you. He wants to open your eyes to what He can do through you once you start walking by faith.

I changed, but not overnight like in those other books you've read. Over years. Slowly and painfully. Sometimes brutally, yet gracefully. The peace I have now is worth every single thing I lost. My story is filled with brokenness, terrible choices, and hideous truths. It is also filled with major comebacks, peace in my soul, and a grace that saved my life.

It is my prayer that *Foolish Faith* will empower you to know that you are nothing short of amazing. You are what people need. You are the change people are praying for. You are the example people delight in. I share my story to attest to the divine resurrecting power of God. To show you that what I thought I could never come back from was entirely and utterly for my good.

Pain made me pray, and prayer made me powerful. Who will you become while waiting?

TRUTH JOURNAL

TRUTH JOURNAL

CHAPTER TWO

TRANSPARENCY IS THE MOTHER OF TRANSFORMATION

> *"I praise you because I am fearfully and wonderfully made; your works are wonderful, I know that full well."*
>
> — Psalms 139:14 New International Version

THE OLDER I get, the more truth and transparency become most important. It's extremely valuable. It's rare. Transparency implies openness, communication, maturity, and personal accountability. We may not realize how much crap we take on a daily basis. If we all learn to filter the noise and instead focus on what is truly authentic, we can get on a better trajectory toward our goals and dreams.

After just two years of marriage, I made the decision to file for divorce. It wasn't a difficult decision for me to make at that moment because the four-year relationship was the most stressful and emotionally draining I'd ever experienced. What was scary was the unknown future that I would walk into. How difficult would life become once I stepped into unchartered waters on my own? I wasn't quite sure if I was ready to challenge my comfort zone, but I knew for certain that my mental, emotional, and spiritual health needed saving. I was dying internally. My marriage was not going to change the way I needed it to, and I could not continue to make a class project out of it any longer. I wanted a comfy, stable life like the one I'd had growing up. I was determined to have that dream even if it meant me going at it alone. But getting back to that dream required me to delve into my past.

The Danger of Low Expectations

I was just a twenty-two-year-old young lady new to Los Angeles, destined to make my mark in Hollywood. I wanted to become an entertainment reporter—attend red carpet events, interview A-list celebrities—the fun stuff. I met one of my best friends, Lova, a fellow Marquette University Alumna, through a networking website, and she assisted me in landing a part-time job as a production assistant at a well-known entertainment network. When I received the job, I moved from Milwaukee, Wisconsin to Los Angeles in ten days. I remember packing up three suitcases and leaving everything else behind because if all else failed, I could simply move back home. The job didn't pay much, but I was so excited to embark on a long-awaited journey that I leaped at the first opportunity to move out of town. I remember lying to my dad, telling him I would earn much more money than what was offered because I feared he wouldn't support my decision to move. I wasn't sure how I was going to make it in Los Angeles working twenty hours a week earning $12.50 an hour. But nothing was going to hold me back. Not even myself. I was determined to discover what I could possibly achieve on my own.

Little did I know that moving to the City of Angels would change my life forever. See…not only did I live in LA, I also lived in La La Land, the land of fairy tales. The white picket fence, a life full of consecutive wins, more ups than downs, no fears or insecurities, and the ultimate comfort level. Everything in Anastasia's world is perfect, all pieces working together cohesively for the best possible outcome. If something seemed to not work, I could repair it, put it back together, add a little glue, and keep it moving. Not this chapter. A life with no mistakes, grief, or pain does not exist for any of us. I grew up a dreamer. As a child, I had a vivid imagination, and I always envisioned myself as this woman of high stature——a joyful and strong woman who had both her home life and career together. The woman all little girls looked up to. I didn't realize that mountains don't rise without earthquakes and that every strong woman overcame her fears and stopped looking back at her mistakes. Somewhere along the way, that woman continued to fade from my sight. As I grew older, this vision blurred as each challenge presented itself, knocking me down, little by little. Eventually, I couldn't stand back up quite as tall as before.

Life was simply okay on the West Coast. If you've ever lived away from home with no family, you understand the transition can be gruesome and downright lonely. There is definitely something to be said about the road to "be-coming" in an unfamiliar place. It's all glitz and glam at first. There's beautiful weather, the laid-back lifestyle, the incredible landscapes, and a myriad of activities and sites to see. Envious of your new life, all your hometown friends and family say, "Wish we were there!" when they tell you how much they miss you. Girl bye, it's rougher than rough! The reality of moving to a new place by yourself is that it's incredibly difficult. It's uncomfortable, expensive, challenging, and oftentimes extremely lonesome. You will have days where you question your move and hide in your desolate lifestyle. You will have days where you want nothing more than the familiarity and comfort of home, friends, family. You will have days you wonder if it will ever truly feel like home and become impatient waiting for everything to finally fall into its proper place. Moving away from home on your own is a unique experience that forces you to uncover new layers and develop an intimate relationship with yourself. You are tested and tried on every level, and when you are pressed against the wall, God will show you just exactly what you are truly made of. Pure gold, honey.

After four months of working part-time, I was offered a full-time position. In my first year, I lived with three different roommates, then I moved out on my own. I was in such a rush to live alone I moved into an apartment in a sketchy neighborhood because I couldn't afford to live anywhere else solo. I think my rent was $825 back then for a one-bedroom unit. However, it was mine, I worked hard for it, and I was at peace. No one bothered me, and I never had to question my safety. Life was good. I was going to church weekly. I was getting back in shape. My social life increased. I loved my job. I was happy. At last, I was beginning to enjoy my life.

I went to a friend's birthday party in Long Beach. At this time, my hours picked up so I didn't go out much, except for work events and really special occasions. I remember being so excited to get out of my apartment just to have some fun. We drank a lot of cocktails, took plenty of pictures, played pool, and danced the night away. That night at the restaurant, I ended up being connected with my future husband. I'm never interested in someone upon first meeting them; perhaps the cocktails got the best of me that night. We exchanged numbers, and there was an instant connection. It would take a couple weeks before we went on our first date. It was close to Christmas, and I flew back home to be with my family. After a few dates, things started to get serious. The conversations increased and so did the visits. I really wasn't looking for anyone at the time. I was content being single. But *this*...this felt good.

This guy was different. He was charming, outgoing, consistent, and was really into me. I got a lot of attention, and I didn't have to ask for things twice. Many of the qualities he had were those I wished I had in myself, which drew me even closer to him. He was my magic. I saw an extension of what I wanted to become. It was what I thought I needed at the moment.

We lived about one hour away from each other, and he would come down every weekend to spend time with me. I thought the effort was admirable. We would talk for hours every day. And although I'm not much of a talker, I enjoyed listening to him. He was a bad boy trying to be good for me. *Chileee...bad boys ain't never been any good.* He had never dated anyone like me, and I believed that because I was a good person and carried myself well that I would get treated differently. I didn't want much; I just enjoyed his company and consistency. With every date, my infatuation for him grew. Every weekend he had a date planned—walks on the beach, dinner, getaways, boat rides, movies, go-kart racing, pool—whatever I liked, he wanted to make happen. I believed he wanted to keep a smile on my face and show me a good time.

He began staying with me over the weekend which eventually became every weekend. Soon, the single life I'd developed for myself shifted. I stopped going to church on Sunday mornings because I was spending time with him. We would usually go out on Saturday nights, and waking up early the next morning became a burden. Eventually, my prayer life stopped as well. I just became so consumed with his presence that nothing else mattered as long as I was with him. If we are not careful, we can be easily distracted. What appears to be a minor concern can shift the entire course of your life. When we think with our feelings and are not cautious, we can miss red flags through our rose-colored lenses.

Why is it that we have a tendency to neglect God when we are happy or when our needs are being met? Why do we forget that we need just as much or even more on our good days than we do on our bad days? But seriously, I believed in God. I prayed. I attended church weekly. The foundation wasn't strong enough. I had the religion, but not the relationship. I didn't have that intimate connection with Him. We do a lot of things based on habit and what we were taught growing up regarding faith. I believe that when we are not truly grounded in our intimate relationship with God, it is very easy to be sidetracked with whatever is going on in our lives. There is a conception that when we are in crisis or feel lost, we pray more, attend church regularly, we even crack open our Bibles and jot down a few Scriptures all with hopes that He'll present Himself. I don't know where you are in your faith walk today, but I know that we all long to be close to Him. But this relationship with Him requires commitment on our part in every phase of our lives, not just our periods in the valley. The same consistency and worship we give Him at rock bottom should be the same, if not more, when we are on the mountaintop. This transformation doesn't happen overnight, but it first begins with daily dedication and responsibility.

If You Can Feel It Why Ask for Proof?

After about four months of dating, we made our relationship official. In my mind, I thought we were moving a little fast considering I had not been single for too long before we met, and I was not exactly sure when he'd ended his last relationship. Truthfully, I didn't ask questions. I didn't want the answer because I didn't want anything to ruin our vibe. I was floating on cloud nine, and I didn't want to be brought back to reality. Our relationship was moving right along without me having to guide it. He began introducing me to his family as his queen. Honey, you couldn't tell me ish!

I started spending time at his place over the weekends. For about nine months, everything was great. I felt nervousness coupled with euphoria. Everything was too good to be true. The infatuation was thrilling and exciting. I didn't have much of a life balance because the relationship took much of my energy and focus. Then suddenly, things changed. It was like day and night. One day I called, and he didn't answer nor call right back like he normally would. We didn't talk on the phone for hours anymore. I remember asking him sadly, "What happened? Why the sudden change?" I can remember him saying it wasn't necessary to talk to me like that every day, and I should just continue to be happy like I had been. He was instantly annoyed that I was questioning the sudden change in his behavior. "What do you want me to say? I'm here, so just leave me alone about it." The effort that I grew accustomed to in the beginning never returned.

Where was this coming from?

Sometimes it's not the people who change, it's the façade that fades. This should have been my cue to exit. I should have bowed out the moment the consistency changed. But at this point, my feelings were too involved. I loved him. Or rather I was in love with the idea of being in love. Or I was in lust, so all of my decision-making was based on emotions and naivety. I honestly knew he was being deceitful and talking to someone else, but I didn't have any proof. I just rolled with it. Eventually, I got used to this new behavior. We still saw each other every weekend. We still went on dates. But there was something different in my gut. I grew worried, frustrated, and irritable. I knew something wasn't right, but I couldn't find the courage to walk away. So I started paying close attention to him. I started checking his phone and social media.

After about a month of snooping, I caught him writing to someone on Facebook. They were making arrangements to see each other, and even being vocal about what was to take place when this meet-up happened. Of course, I snapped on him. He claimed that she wanted him and he didn't want her and that I should stop being insecure. The typical lies. I was angry. I cried, and I knew that wasn't the truth, and yet I stayed. I knew he was lying straight to my face. But in hindsight I realized I'd rather be played later than disappointed at that moment, so I continued on with him. I was silly. I allowed nine good months with him to convince me that it wasn't necessary to walk away. That maybe it was just a *small* mistake. I was so caught up with ensuring that his crown never slipped that I became totally oblivious when his mask did. Don't convince yourself into committing to a man while he takes his time deciding whether or not he wants to commit to you. We must learn to trust our instincts. We want to give the person we love the benefit of the doubt. We believe that we have to give them a second chance. We don't want our emotions, time, and love wasted. We don't want to feel foolish. We feel that we need to fight for what we want. We must trust ourselves first before attempting to extend that trust to someone else. The greatest gift God ever gave you is your intuition. Our spirit will never lie to us, so we never need to wait for the physical manifestation of what we're thinking.

Today, I am a woman who believes that if a man shows me that he is not a man of his word, then I will show him a woman who is no longer interested. A lack of follow-through is one of the quickest ways I will lose interest. When a man does not back up his work or actions, read that message clearly. And if you think it's not a big deal, you are sadly mistaken. The biggest mistake I've made throughout my twenties was that I didn't trust myself. I didn't trust my intuition. I gave a lot of people the benefit of the doubt and allowed them to withdraw my energy even when they didn't deserve it. And since I wasn't sure of who I was or where I was headed in this phase of my life, I became influenced by the thoughts and opinions of others.

What God sends you will arrive in clarity, not confusion. There is never a need to rush into love. Don't accept love that requires you to suffer first in hopes to be glorified later. The biggest red flag God sends is the absence of peace. Whatever is meant to be will always find its way. And when it's not, it will cause you to have insecurity, doubt, and stress. It is not a requirement to give someone second, third, or fourth chances. We ignore truths for temporary happiness. It's so easy for someone to be exactly what you need them to

> **Don't accept love that requires you to suffer first in hopes to be glorified later.**

be for a couple weeks, a month, or even several months. But people can't pretend long.

Over the years, I questioned myself over and over again. Why did I not leave at this moment? He wasn't a bad guy; he just wasn't for me. And that is okay. Why did I feel the need to hold it together? I had so many answers—loneliness (remember, I was in a new city and didn't have any support in town), insecurity, and fear. He instantly became my rock in this new world of mine, and I had a dependence on him. He was my security blanket.

The biggest reason why women give chances to undeserving men is that we don't know who we are; that's why we don't feel like we are worthy of great things. We don't believe we deserve to be valued. If you don't hold yourself to a high standard, you can very much assume that the standards of those around you are low. If you do the bare minimum for yourself, you're vibrating on a lower frequency; therefore, your energy signals to others that you're willing to accept anything. Your job is not to convince other people to love you. Your job is to love yourself and attract someone on the level you're on. You are in charge of your own vibration. Raise it, adjust it, cleanse it, but never lower it for someone else. Once you increase the standard for yourself, you will begin to attract that kind of partner into your life. Are you compromising your standards just to have a significant other or friends so that you don't feel alone? Over the next few chapters, we will discuss how a season of singleness is one of the best things that could ever happen to you and how vital it is to not waste it. If you are not alone, it is time to qualify your relationships. When you know and understand what you have to bring to the table, you can bring out the receipts anytime someone questions your worth. You have a platform to expect reciprocity. You know your worth and will abide by the values that you've set. Figure out exactly who you are so you will never again settle for less than what you truly deserve.

Calling you daily, opening the car door, paying for dates, kissing your forehead, and asking if you made it home safely is not grounds to be in a relationship. It is not conducive. He may be nice; there are a lot of nice men in this world. We have got to stop jumping for decent men instead of waiting for great ones. Don't allow anyone to trick you into becoming low maintenance in an effort to become more desirable. There is a difference between low maintenance and low standards. In order for a woman to be low maintenance, there has to be a high standard when it comes to how a man treats you. When he is consistently operating from a higher standard, it is low maintenance because it's the norm. If the people around you don't hold

> **We have got to stop jumping for decent men instead of waiting for great ones.**

themselves to a high standard, they will not be able to stay in your life. They will either have to rise to meet you where you are or exit stage left because the pressure will be far too great to endure. They will consistently question what you have to offer, and you will be considered "high maintenance," "too good," or "snobby" because you're asking for more than that person is capable of providing. Stop confusing standards with preferences and your assertiveness of these standards as being "too much" because a man's criticism is rooted in his inability to perform and deliver.

How they treat you is much more important than how much you like them. Therefore, your self-respect must be stronger than your feelings.

TRUTH JOURNAL

TRUTH JOURNAL

CHAPTER THREE

I ONLY LOST ONE THING I EVER WANTED BACK...MYSELF

"Whoever finds their life will lose it, and whoever loses their life for my sake will find it."

— Matthew 10:39 New International Version

WHEN I CLOSE my eyes and envision who I am, I see two different versions: the version of my past and the version that I am blossoming into. Neither are full expressions of who I have potential to become, but they all are true in some regard. On one side, I see a young, shy girl who is nervous about the future, yet she pretends she is okay. She looks confident on the outside, but a bit insecure on the inside. She is afraid of being judged. You would believe that she has it together, but in actuality, she doesn't want to be seen and just wants to live under the radar. She is scared of what others may think of her. She is unsure if she can overcome, if she'll ever get her life back on track. She doesn't know her potential. Her soul is lost, and her heart is heavy. The only thing she wants is to be happy again.

The other version is a woman who is fully confident and has taken control of her circumstances. Her past does not haunt her anymore because she knows the strength that she gained is directly correlated to the pain she has experienced. She is at peace with herself and her journey. She is in love with living an authentic life. Her heart is giving, and she is committed to assisting any woman who shares similar experiences. She has learned that her superpower is being fearlessly transparent, and she is no longer bound from the thoughts and opinions of others. She is powerful because she doesn't allow doubts and fears to keep her from letting the world see who she is. She is proof that you can walk through hell and still be an angel. God's mercy has given her an undeniable grace. I needed both versions of myself to get me to where I am today. Neither could exist without the other.

Own Your Scars, For in Due Time They Will Set You Free

Can I have a moment of honesty here? So I've given myself a little over three months to complete my first draft of *Foolish Faith*. I don't know how many chapters I will end up with. I am assuming somewhere around nine or ten. I've given myself a week to write and edit each chapter as I go along, leaving me with a couple weeks at the end of my timeline to look it over and make any changes. I am a Virgo, so I need to schedule everything. We are detailed individuals. It keeps us sane.

Anyway, I am on the second week of writing this chapter. It's difficult. And it shouldn't be because I'm simply describing my own life. But last week, I just couldn't get anything out. I am reading my diary cringing, unsure of which details to add. I became terrified again. I had excuse after excuse, and I felt more tired than usual. I busied myself with other things, anything that could take me away from writing this, and ultimately, it would take me one month to complete this chapter. Honestly, I am nervous about sharing what is to come. Maybe I'll abort the mission, remove the painful details, and get straight to the pretty parts. Doing so is the road that will lead me away from possible shame. However, pushing myself beyond the shame will lead me toward ultimate freedom. Sharing your truth in an intimate setting is totally different than sharing with the world. One day, my daughter will read this. I pray that I will have made her proud. When we want to kick things up to another level, the enemy uses our daily circumstances to delay our progression. And because we haven't yet learned to conquer fear, we succumb to it. I said a prayer and asked God, "What should I write here?" and He told me to just keep it real.

That weekend as I was writing, Tyler Perry had his star-studded gala at the new Tyler Perry Studios. I became inspired. While looking through each and every post on social media, awing each photo like I hadn't already seen that same picture five minutes ago, I came across a video from Tyler's acceptance speech at the 2019 BET Awards. At the end of the speech, he said, "There are people connected to your dream; people are waiting on you to help them cross." That statement resonated with me to my core as I navigated this chapter of my life. The thing is your fear of looking foolish is holding you back. You can literally overthink yourself right out of a miracle. Just surrender, move your feet, and let God do what He does.

God, Please Use the Broken Pieces of My Life to Build Something for Your Glory. Amen.

Listen...I know we are all tired of making mistakes. We just want to get there—the other side of all the pain we've endured. Where we have more wins than losses. If I fall down, I can figure it out, learn my lessons, and just move on to the next. How many of us just wished that God would sit next to us on our beds and tell us exactly what to do or tell us exactly what will happen? So much could be avoided. I trust there have been moments in your life too where you wished you could rewind the time. The famous saying is, "If only I knew back then what I know now."

Let me tell you what I wish I had known. I wish I would have known how to have the courage to confidently walk away from anything that did not serve me well.

I continued to date my boyfriend. I continued to shield myself from not seeing the real, authentic truth in who he was. And because I believed in potential more than reality, I subconsciously sacrificed my own growth in order to help him advance.

I still didn't trust him.

And even though I found proof the first time he cheated, it wasn't enough. If he apologized, then I can give him another chance, right? When you give an unworthy person chances, you never feel at ease; you become obsessed. I remember going out with my co-workers and friends less and less. I made excuses, saying I had plans with my boyfriend. It wasn't the truth. His weekend stays at my place turned into four, five days a week. It was so I knew where he was. I thought I felt more comfortable, but I was really manipulative and controlling. Happiness turned into anxiety. And what was initially fun became a chore. Although he said he would never do it again, I was going to ensure that wouldn't happen again by forcing him to be in my presence.

Over the next six months, our relationship would hit a few high points, but also some major lows.

My restlessness grew to an all-time high. I knew what would put an end to this. I did the unthinkable. All of my friends, cousins, and even I had our fair share of "relationship crazy." We would laugh and joke about this quite often, but none of them have ever done what I did.

I snuck an app on his phone.

Yes, I did it. In the middle of the night as he slept. The best time to catch a cheater in action.

Sure did.

The app showed on my phone his messages, call logs, even voicemails. It also included the phone numbers. It was hidden on his phone so he couldn't trace it.

Boom, there you have it!

Less than twenty-four hours after I installed the app, I discovered he was in a relationship. A WHOLE OTHER RELATIONSHIP with a woman he was on and off with for years. I can laugh at this today, but at that moment, I was crushed. I watched their conversation before I said anything. At this point, I was done. But before I told him that I knew, I decided to call the girl. Not to argue, but because I want to hear her side of the story. You know, to come to her as a woman...HA! Yeah, I've been there before. I started to dial, but I got scared. I wasn't sure if I was ready to hear the details. I backed off. I knew what I'd read. I knew what I felt. I was at his apartment waiting on him to return. Should I stay? Should I say anything at all? Ugh, I was pissed. I paced back and forth debating if I should wait or not. I should have left, but where's the fun in that?

As soon as he entered the front door, I said, *"So you in multiple relationships I see."*

Him: *"Huh?"*

"You think you slick. You didn't think I was gonna find out about this chick?"

I didn't give him a chance to respond or tell me another lie...I left. I slammed the door and hopped right in my car. He didn't try to stop me, follow, or plead for me to stay. On my hour drive back to LA, I was watching the app. I saw that he was calling her phone. Not mine. My heart was officially broken. *Why is he not chasing me? Why is he not coming after me?* I loved him, I always did right by him, and I could not understand why this was happening. I was able to withhold my tears during that ride home, but as soon as I stepped into my apartment, I fell flat on my face in my bed and cried more tears than I knew existed.

I called my best friend, Asha, to tell her what happened. Of course, in typical BFF fashion, we decided to call the girl on three-way. As the phone rang, my nerves had gotten really bad, and my fingers and lips were trembling.

"Hello."

"Um, hello. May I speak to..."

"*This is she.*"

"My name is Anastasia. I wanted to talk to you about..."

"*I've actually been trying to reach out to you.*"

I was like, "What??" She knew exactly who I was. This was already too much for my nerves.

"*I've known him for about five years now. We got back together three months ago.*"

She also lived about an hour away from him, so she visited him during the week on her off days. I saw him on the weekend. Easy enough.

"He had gotten me pregnant, but I just had an abortion."

"And you truly wanted to go through with that?"

"I'm not ready for another child at the moment. We usually have these moments where we fall off, but we will never completely stop talking."

"Hmm. Oh, is that right? We'll see about that."

We hung up. Asha asked, "Well...how do you feel?"

"Umm...I don't know. I just...I just feel really sad right now."

He finally called me.

"I spoke to..."

"Really?!?"

"So what do you think she told me?"

"...well, I mean...It's really not like that. It's not what you think at all. I really don't want her."

"Clearly it is exactly what I think it is!"

"What are you trying to say...this is it? You're done with me?"

"Yes, I am. I refuse to allow you to continue to play me for a fool."

A few days passed by, and he didn't call to apologize. After about a week, I called him. I was angry. I forced an apology out of him. I knew it wasn't sincere, but I just needed to hear something. During all this, my grandmother passed away in Wisconsin. I flew back home to attend her funeral. While I was there, I didn't speak to him. I didn't tell anyone what happened because I was embarrassed. I made a plea to myself that I wouldn't speak to him anymore. He did reach out, but I didn't answer while I was away.

Once I returned to LA, it was getting close to Valentine's Day. I didn't want to be alone. I got antsy. I initiated a conversation. Chileee...SMH. I texted him to ask if he would come spend that day with me. He said he wouldn't be able to; he had to work, and he also had his son. He was an entrepreneur, so I believed he was busy, but he also could have taken off. He always did when *he* wanted to, anyway. I was really sad that he wasn't fighting for me. I knew it wasn't working, but I could not pull myself away from the relationship. The insecurity in me wanted to see why he could not do right by me. I prayed to God that night to give me the strength and courage to leave him because my tears and my frustration didn't motivate him to change. He didn't want to. In my mind, I made a conscious decision that I was done with him.

Things every woman needs to come to terms with:

- Stop begging undeserving men to get their act together.
- No response is a response.
- If they wanted to, they would.
- Timing will not always be in your favor.
- Not everyone will have the same heart as you.

We know when we deserve more than what we are settling for. Women have been taught that love is about longevity and sacrifice. In turn, we stay beyond the expiration date, and we sacrifice more than we knew we had. There are standards and boundaries you should not waver on just to be in a long-term relationship or marriage. Learn when to exit! As a woman, your most important asset is your self-worth and the second is your time. Your value begins with you. DO NOT discount yourself. The moment you decide to settle, you get even less than what you settled for.

> **The moment you decide to settle, you get even less than what you settled for.**

Hunniii, trust me, it hurts to lose control. You're believing and praying for the best, giving it all you've got, to then being confronted that it was all a lie. The first thing the enemy does is make you feel at fault.

"What could I have done to make it different?"

"Was I not worth anything?"

"Why did I waste so much time?"

You begin to cry tears, wondering what areas you've failed. Tonight as I type this, God is sending me to tell you...

"You have done everything you could. You demonstrated your character by being loving, genuine, and real. They showed theirs by being deceitful, dishonest, and manipulative."

Oftentimes, we view heartbreak as a loss when in reality, losing unnecessary weight is a gain. God reveals disloyalty to bring you clarity, and there are always clues before destruction. You betray yourself when you ignore the red flags your intuition makes you privy to. Trust yourself, believe what He shows you, and move forward alone.

Self-betrayal while dating may look like this:

- Consistently changing your schedule to fit theirs
- Making excuses for behavior that has been upsetting to you
- Agreeing to things you truly don't agree with
- Ignoring your needs to seem easygoing
- Doing most of the work to get it to "work"
- Moving more quickly than you'd like out of fear that you'll be rejected if you don't
- "Letting it go" when you've been hurt or violated
- Agreeing to less than what you truly want or need

If you wait for the best in anything you desire in life, you can and will have it. Loving yourself is an art that no one else can give you. You can't expect from others what you don't have the capacity to create for yourself. I've chosen to love me first. So I never have to depend on others to do what I should do for myself.

It's okay to fight for someone who loves you. It's not okay to fight for someone *to* love you. There is a huge difference. Real love is peaceful, it puts your heart at ease. You trust it. You believe in it. It's free. Free to grow into whatever it desires. It's no longer free when you have the urge to control it. And you don't trust what you need to control.

I spent Valentine's Day alone. I bought myself flowers and even a pair of bomb pumps. I ordered takeout, and I even went to the gym that night because in my mind, I was already focused on my "revenge body." I knew I was hurting deep down inside, and I simply hoped that I would fall out of love with what was not for me.

At around 2 a.m., I received a phone call, a pre-recorded message from jail.

"This call will be recorded and monitored. I have a call from—, an inmate at a Riverside County detention facility..."

Yep, it was him. I popped right up because I wanted to hear what happened.

"What are you doing?"

"What do you mean what I'm doing? It's 2 a.m..."

"Yeah...so uh, I got a DUI."

"I wonder how that happened, and you told me you had to work."

"I did work. Then I went to go see my cousin..."

"So you found the time you said you didn't have."

"I know, I'm not shit for that. Had I come down there, I wouldn't be here. I'm really sorry. I'll be out in a few hours. I'll call you then."

I experienced more disappointment than happiness dealing with this man. For one, he said he had to work. Two, he said he would have his son. And three, had he been interested in spending time with me, he would not have been in the situation. Once he was released, he called me at around ten in the morning while I was at work.

"I know you're upset. You asked me to be there with you, and I had an excuse. I feel like I failed you."

"You didn't fail me; you failed yourself."

"All I could think about was that I should have done things differently, not just this situation, but everything."

"Differently how?"

"I know that I don't always show it, but I don't want to lose you. You mean everything to me. You deserve better than me, but I'm willing to do any and everything to show you that I can be who you need me to be. I don't know what you are going to say, but I really don't want to lose you. I can make Valentine's Day up to you. I'll make it all up to you. I really want you to be my wife."

"What did you just say?"

"This isn't a proposal because you deserve better than this. But I do want to ask you one day soon with a ring. All I ask is that you give me another chance. I don't want you to leave."

"I really appreciate that, but I don't know what to say. I think we will really just have to see."

"Being in there really just has me thinking differently and about what really matters."

As ridiculous as that was, and as foolish as I was, I could not believe what I was hearing! He was never an emotional type of person. He never expressed himself in this manner.

I paused for a few seconds and thought to myself, Is he serious? I guess I can see where this goes.

Even though I didn't show it, I was sort of happy. I'll admit it. I pretended to sound nonchalant, but deep down, I was pleasantly surprised. I immediately remembered the prayer I'd said before. I was prepared to leave him, and at that time I just knew God had brought him back to me. I wasn't even thinking about marriage. I couldn't believe I had an answer that fast. Or so *I thought*.

Girl, after work I went to my apartment, packed some clothes, hopped on the 10 freeway, and went to see him. Just that fast. From this point on, I practically moved in with him. I stayed at his place several nights a week, and I only stopped by my apartment to grab what I needed. I wanted to see if he was *really* going to change.

Two months went by. We were in a really good space. Like really good. The other girl was gone; she was never an issue again. I was just happy that it appeared I had gotten what I asked for. That all my time and efforts were not in vain. That I didn't have to start over. That he saw I really loved him. We were happier than we had ever been. He was open. He communicated more. He was more thoughtful than I'd ever experienced him to be. I thought maybe the jail thing had changed him. How could I not think this wasn't God? What I truly wanted was happening. And happening fast.

In four months, he proposed to me...at his place...totally off guard. We were watching a movie. I got up to make myself a cocktail, and when I came back, there he was on his knee with a ring. His voice and hands were shaky.

I meant what I said. I want you to be my wife. I'm willing to prove myself over and over and over again for your love. Will you marry me?

You know I said yes.

We kissed and sat back on the sofa. I continued to look at my hand. I couldn't believe this was happening.

I did not shed a single tear.

I was nervous.

I didn't tell my mom until two days later. I debated putting it on Facebook. Because...you know it ain't real unless you post it. HA! I didn't tell my homegirls right away. I remember being happy, but not as happy as I should have been. I wasn't ecstatic. I didn't shout, "I'm a FEYONCE!" from the mountaintop. Something was wrong. It didn't sit right with me. I knew it wasn't right, but I thought how *bad* could it be? I mean no person is *that* bad, and if for whatever reason they were, I could always get divorced. That was a real statement I made to myself.

We began planning for a wedding almost immediately. If you've ever been married, you know planning a wedding takes on a life of its own, and I lost myself in it. Searching for venues took the pressure off a rocky relationship. We found a beautiful charter yacht in Newport Beach, and the moment we stepped foot on it, we knew it was the one. Three levels, with decks on each one, it was certified boss status.

We sat with the wedding coordinator, signed the contract the same day, and set a date for exactly one year out. As much as I loved cake tastings, picking out décor, and ordering pretty invitations, I shied away from asking myself the real hard questions. After everything that happened in this relationship, were we truly ready to get married? Even though I believed God sent my answer, that didn't take away the work that needed to be done.

I never did the work. I planned for a wedding and never planned for a marriage.

I didn't want to. I wanted to live in what I thought was bringing me happiness and not what was real. That bubbly feeling in my gut came back again. This time, I asked him to come to pre-marital counseling with me. At this point, we were maybe five months out from the wedding. I knew we needed it. He agreed. He came with me to two sessions then stopped. He felt that he did not need to go. My anxiety grew. He became hostile about counseling. We even argued over it.

Stacey, why did you not call this off? Why did you not make this a non-negotiable? Why are you still in this toxic relationship?

I was in it too deep. All of my family lived out of town, and many had purchased their flights. Truthfully, whatever they lost in airfare wouldn't compare to a potential lifetime of heartache. I was scared. I was attached. I didn't want to go through the process of a breakup and be alone again. His bullshit became my normal. I was so caught up in the engagement roller coaster that I didn't notice myself spiraling out of control.

Truth is, I didn't want him to be with the other girl. I wanted to win. We'd both put in time and effort, but I didn't want to lose what I brought to the relationship. This was a game, and Stacey never loses. I completely lost sight of me being the prize and put him on a pedestal. We'd never work as a real couple, and deep down, I knew that. But I wasn't ready to face myself. Or the truth.

Do you really want the life you're currently fighting for?

TRUTH JOURNAL

TRUTH JOURNAL

_____
_____
_____
_____
_____
_____
_____
_____
_____
_____
_____
_____
_____
_____
_____
_____
_____
_____
_____
_____

CHAPTER FOUR

YOU CAN BE THE ONE HE MARRIES AND STILL GET PLAYED

> "All of us have sinned and fallen short of God's glory. But God treats us much better than we deserve, and because of Christ Jesus, He freely accepts us and sets us free from our sins."
>
> — Romans 3:23-24
> Contemporary English Version

HAVE YOU EVER received valuable advice from someone, and you know you should listen but decide to do your own thing anyway?

Because how bad could it really, truly get?

I don't think I've ever said anything so crazy to myself.

My cousin, Danishia, and I have gotten very close over the years. She probably knows every single thing about me. She's given me invaluable advice and has always supported me regardless of my decision to go through with the marriage or not. But this time, I could tell she was concerned. She knew I was caught up in the hype.

Once she asked me, "Are you preparing for this marriage in the same way you are preparing for the wedding?"

"*I mean, well, yes, of course. Why wouldn't I be?*" I was oblivious because distractions don't look like distractions while they're distracting you.

As time neared closer to our wedding, my uncertainty grew. I was unsure if I really wanted to go through with it all. I was scared. But in my mind, I couldn't cancel. Family and friends from out-of-state had booked their accommodations. They were so excited to be a part of one of my biggest moments, and I was contemplating if I would be a runaway bride. I couldn't fathom postponing and wasting all their money. Even more so, I didn't want to look like a joke. It's so silly, but I truly cared about what people would think. To have planned this entire wedding, documented the whole process, just to say in the end, "*Sooo we decided to hold off on getting married*" was embarrassing.

"*If you're that nervous about it, we can just have a big party instead,*" Danishia said.

"Girl, byeeee. I mean maybe it's just my nerves getting the best of me."

"*I don't know if I believe that,*" she replied with worry.

I thought to myself, *No one knows you better than YOU. Stop choosing other people's 'opinion' over the 'knowing' in your gut.* I knew deep down inside that I needed to cancel this wedding. One day, I even said I would call everyone and let them know that we were just going to wait. I swallowed my pride. I had to make a hard decision.

Stacey,

Girl...leave that man alone. If it doesn't feel right, it probably isn't. Yes, you love him. But he is not ready for the kind of love you bring to the table.

Anastasia

I sat at our dining table with my notebook of contacts. I stared at the notebook for hours.

I mean, like really...how bad could it be? If things went south, we can try counseling again. If we just can't figure it out, we can get divorced.

I was still happy in the relationship. The changes he promised me he was doing. He was consistent. He was thoughtful. He appeared to be more at ease about the wedding than I was. So I sat down with him and asked again. *Maybe if I ask just one more time, I'll feel a little better.*

"Hey, how are you feeling?" I asked, looking for some sort of validation.

"*Pretty good, how are you?*" He knew something was up.

"I'm okay. We're almost here. In the homestretch now."

"*I know, I'm ready. I'm excited.*"

"You're excited?" I questioned.

"Yeah, you're the only one who isn't."

"Wait, why do you say that?"

"You're the only one walking around here like you're confused about it."

"Are you not nervous?"

"I mean, yeah, a little. Who wouldn't be? But I meant what I said, and I still feel the same way."

I married him.

Against everything I said. Against everything I feared. The doubts never ceased. But I loved him. So I followed my heart and not my mind.

We had a beautiful wedding. I couldn't believe I was someone's wife. It all happened so fast. The entire day was a blur. At the end of our night back at the suite, we ate chocolate dipped strawberries and tried to recap our perfect day. As we opened a few of our gifts, anxiety consumed me, and I began thinking to myself...

I hope I did the right thing.

God, I really just hope I made the right choice.

Over and over, I repeated this. In order to not cave into those emotions, I also told myself, *Well, I mean, how bad can it really be anyway?*

The weekend was over. It was time to return home. Wedding vibes faded, and everything went back to normal. I'll be honest, the excitement immediately left. I was not excited about being married anymore. I had gotten what I thought I wanted, but I really truly *didn't* want it. I knew that I'd settled.

I felt like I was carrying a bag of bricks in my gut. I shouldn't have done this. Two weeks into the marriage, we were already arguing. *Here we go.* I should have known better. But I didn't.

After It Expires It's No Longer Good for You. This Ain't About Food.

I began to search for new jobs because I desperately needed a change. I gave up my apartment two months before the wedding, and I moved all my belongings in with him. I was commuting two hours each way from the Inland Empire to LA, and the distance started to drain me. As I prepared to land a new gig, I scheduled doctor and dentist appointments in case I wouldn't have medical insurance right away at my new position. I took a day off work, went to see my dentist, and I got an annual pap smear with my gynecologist.

A week later, I was sitting at my desk at work and my cell phone rang.

"*Hello, Anastasia, this is Doctor…I am calling to tell you that we've received your results from your pap smear, and you tested positive for chlamydia.*"

"Excuse me?!" I snapped.

She made an appointment for a follow-up visit. I immediately called him. I couldn't even dial the number because I was so pissed off.

"Clearly, I'm the fool because you still sleeping around, and now I got chlamydia."

There was silence.

"Oh, so now you not gonna say nothing?!"

"*That can't be possible...*" he hesitantly replied.

"So I'm the liar?! Am I lying now? I must be because I've been lying to myself about your ass all along!"

I couldn't even get through the rest of my day. To think at my appointment, I told my doctor I'd just gotten married. I was so embarrassed. I left work early. I knew this was all a mistake, and I thought to myself repeatedly that this was what I signed up for.

On my way to the house, he called. He was calm. He offered an apology. I think that if what he said was genuine, I would remember. But whatever it was, it wasn't honest. *He was not honest.* He claimed that this happened prior to us getting married. Since we'd wed, he had not slept with anyone. I had no proof, no call logs, text messages, or anything. I wasn't looking. I gave that up. However, I simply knew it was all lies.

This happened on our two-month anniversary. I wanted to leave, but frankly, I was scared. I was ashamed. I knew I could not do this anymore. I couldn't blame anyone but myself. I wanted to ask, *Why is God taking me through this?* But clearly, God never told me to marry this man even if that's what I believed He showed me. I couldn't tell anybody what I was going through. I couldn't even put him out because I couldn't afford our rent by myself. I also didn't have the money to move out on my own. I was too embarrassed to ask my parents for help because, truth is, I shouldn't have married him in the first place. So I stayed. I never told a soul what happened.

I suggested we go to counseling. He agreed. The first session went horribly. Instead of discussing the situation, he flipped it on me and how I complained so much. Our counselor agreed with him! Yes, I did complain, and in hindsight, it was because we were never meant to be together. I spent a lot of time trying to mold him into a version of himself that had never existed. I believed that as much as he put me through, he should compensate for his actions. He should have worked extra hard to earn my trust back. Our therapist explained that I needed to either forgive and move on or leave. Although this may have been true, he took her suggestions as if he was off the hook. Needless to say, because I was to blame, he didn't think he needed any more counseling sessions. Even when I attempted to voice my concerns, I could never get through to him because he would always retaliate under the guise of 'Remember what our therapist said.' I continued counseling by myself. I continued with the same woman. Why? Because I knew she would give me the advice I needed to hear despite the horrific first counseling session.

"This is who he is, and you must take it for face value. Quit thinking you can love him into being a better man, because you can't," she told me in my first solo session.

I needed to make a decision to either find happiness in who he'd shown me to be or leave. No more complaining. She thought he would do whatever necessary to please himself with no regard to anyone else. I took that to heart. I continued therapy alone because I needed something to keep me sane while I figured out what I was going to do. I was not in a good space financially, and I didn't have anywhere to go.

As I continued in therapy, I began praying to God to change my husband. I wanted God to change him because at the end of the day, I had taken a vow. I'd invested so much of myself. As much as I had hoped that this was a 'phase,' a big part of me did not believe things would change. Things would get worse.

My spirit was broken. I started going to church alone. If I was going to stay, I had to change my perspective. At one point, I put only positivity into our marriage. I spoke positively. I forced myself to be happy. Things did start to shift. We started getting along. Our conversations became more fluid. We laughed together more often. One evening, I even came home to a bubble bath, candles, a glass of wine, and the book I was reading placed in the bathroom. Something as simple as that really put a smile on my face.

I was still applying for a new job. I wanted something closer to where we lived, and I wanted something that I would enjoy doing. I was at a turning point in my life and career. Entertainment was no longer a passion, and I needed a new beginning. I believed a fresh start would give me a sense of renewed energy. My husband suggested that I get my real estate license. He knew I loved looking at homes, interior décor, and watching HGTV. I signed up for an online course and passed the state examination. Six months after beginning my job search, I found a job as an event coordinator at a university close to our home. I was excited. I hoped that my sacrifice of changing my life to fit this new one *we* created would show my husband that I was serious about my family, and hopefully, he would follow my lead.

Yet even with all this, I couldn't find it in me to be happy. I tried my hardest to settle into whatever this marriage was, but I couldn't fake it any longer. I was drained. I would get enough sleep each night, and I still woke up fatigued. It was my *soul* that was tired.

Truthfully, I never got over the infidelity. I forced myself to believe that I was. I experienced a lot of anxiety. I convinced myself to believe this life was okay. I didn't feel comfortable in my relationship. I couldn't speak or express myself to him in ways I had in the past. I did not feel I could ever fully be happy. I was an honest and true wife. But I knew this was not a 'til death do we part' marriage. It was only a matter of time.

Nothing hurts worse than knowing you settled. I made a decision to settle. And now I was paying the consequences because he could not rise to what I needed him to be. I hoped that if I changed, maybe he would as well. I was asking him to do something that he was not capable of. Why did I want him to follow my lead anyway? I deserve a man who knows when and how to take the lead. One person cannot carry a two-person relationship. It becomes heavy very quickly. A relationship should be reciprocal.

Stacey,

I can tell you over and over to leave the situation, but you won't until you are ready. One day, you will wake up and realize that this isn't what you want to feel like anymore. Then you will be done. You are always in control. You don't have to wait for someone to tell you where things are going. The decision is yours.

Anastasia

By our one-year anniversary, our relationship was null and void. We both recognized that our marriage was failing and could not be restored. We'd had some good times, but the bad definitely outweighed the good. Instead of incessantly blaming one another for our dissatisfaction with each other, we started spending much of our time apart.

You Get Exactly What You Ask For, and Then You Realize You've Got to Get Better at Asking

Shortly after our anniversary, we moved into his mother's house. He had gotten into major trouble, and we immediately needed to move out of our house. He was in a partnership of a marijuana dispensary and had fallen out with one of his partners over money.

"Hello...bae." There was a quiver in his voice.

"Yeah."

"What are you doing? Are you sitting down?"

"What are you talking about?!" I was upset because I don't like surprises.

"Um...so. Someone just shot up our house."

Yes, you read that right. Straight shot up our home. In broad daylight.

Me:...

"Hello...hello."

"Did you say what I think you said?!"

I was at work at the time. I worked the second shift, and I had just clocked in when this happened. I was actually debating on calling in sick that day, but something didn't sit right, and I went in anyway. He was actually outside in our front yard when this all took place. Fearing the safety of his son and me, we moved to his mother's house.

Against my word, he decided to use our home as a place to trim the cannabis plants that grew in the dispensary. There was a drastic change in him. His demeanor and attitude was different. I knew that he had completely lost his mind. I couldn't quite put my finger on what it was, but he never made *these* types of decisions. He was never this foolish. We fought long and hard about how dangerous and flat-out stupid this was. He was extremely stubborn, and once his mind was made up, there was no changing it. I am similar in that way. Two days before my 27th birthday, he got a call in the middle of the night from one of his friends telling him he needed to get to the house ASAP. I begged him not to go. I couldn't hear the conversation, but I knew it was bad. I prayed that nothing would happen to him. As much as I resented him, I didn't want to imagine the worst possible outcome from this.

Our home was robbed.

He was set up *again*. Men with guns forced entry into our home, tied up and pistol whipped those that were there trimming his cannabis. Then they stole what was left of our belongings, including all of the plants.

He came back to his mother's house in a panic. He had a large safe at the house. Inside was more marijuana and money. They could not move it, nor pop it open, and he needed to grab what was left. His stepfather went into his own safe and grabbed the guns. The whole house piled into the truck, and each person had a gun in hand. Including me.

This is the part of my story that I was most afraid of telling. I went back and forth for months asking God, "Is this even necessary?" I stopped writing for a very long time over these details. I didn't think I would ever have the courage. But I promised myself if I was going to do this, nothing was off limits.

What in the world was going on with my life? This is nothing close to how I was raised. NOT. EVEN. CLOSE. Never ever in my entire life have I ever been so scared of something happening to me. We pulled up to our house, and I hopped into the front seat with his mom as the guys went inside. As my fingers clutched the magazine of the Smith & Wesson .45, I cried. I wasn't sure if I would make it back to his mother's house that night. All I wanted was for God to spare my life.

The coast stayed clear, and he got everything from the safe. No one was at the house. We were in and out within a few minutes then headed back to his mother's house. I had no words, but the tears that flowed down my face in the car displayed everything I was feeling inside. The car ride back was silent. For them, they would never speak of this moment again, and for me, I was completely, utterly flustered.

We circled his mom's neighborhood a few times before we pulled up. It was still silent. His mom took back her gun that was lying on my shaky lap. She wiped it down, placed it back in her bag, looked at me with a slight nod, and we exited the car. He went upstairs, lay in bed, and started crying. He locked himself in the bedroom for two full days. Depression overtook him. He was defeated. He believed he just wanted to provide better for his family. Although I resented him, I kept my 'I told you so's' to myself. I kept my distance until he was ready to talk.

He wanted to go to church. Yes…church. All this time, I'd been going alone. Now he wanted to accompany me. He joined the church that Sunday and even planned to get baptized again. Cute, but I was over it. I needed time to come up with a plan so I could get a place of my own and move out. I wanted to be nice. I wanted to be supportive, helpful, and all that I had been since we first began dating. I wanted to comfort him in his time of pain, but at this point, I had nothing left to give. I could have been home and outside with him when the shooting happened. His child could have been there when that happened. I understand the game and what comes with it, but the relationship was not worth it any longer. He was not worth it any longer.

I couldn't call and tell my mom about this. Girl, please. She would definitely try to make me move back home. I didn't even think about telling my dad. That was just not going to happen. As I write this, he still doesn't know and won't find out until he reads this book. This was all too much. On any given day, it's still just too much for any person to experience.

I wasn't safe with him. I believed he would protect me from a stranger, but after the infidelity, the STD, and now this, I lacked total trust in him. I began to have a rush of adrenaline. It would reappear at various moments. The fight-or-flight feeling. That if I didn't move quickly, I could put myself in even more danger. I believed that something could actually happen to me. I knew I needed to end this marriage. I didn't want God to be displeased with me for getting divorced, but I could not live the rest of my life like this. I was miserable. I was resentful. I was angry with myself for being so foolish.

FOOLISH FAITH

It's Okay to Outgrow the Life You Thought You Wanted

It was six months to the day that we moved in with his mom. It was a Sunday. I went to church with his cousin and received a message that would change everything. I remember it as if it were yesterday. The pastor asked us to pray to God for three miracles to happen by the following Sunday. He began praying, and everyone bowed their heads, making their requests known to God. I prayed that God would either miraculously restore my marriage or give me the way out. I prayed for a place to live, to be safe and away from any harm. I was so nervous because I'd never prayed like this before. I'd said many prayers regarding our relationship, but I had never asked God to continuously show me if he should be in my life. Had I actually included Him from the beginning, I likely wouldn't have been here to begin with.

Stacey,

When you do not start your process with God at the center, it will always end in disappointment.

Anastasia

After church, I went about my day as usual. I was already in the process of organizing my things, so when I found myself an apartment, everything I had would already be together. He was gone when I returned from church. His cousin stopped by to check on him.

"He said he was on his way back from Riverside from --- house. I figured he would be here by now."

I immediately knew that was a lie because I knew where that friend lived, and it ain't over there. Remember that tracking app I mentioned earlier? Even though I'd removed it from my phone, it was still on his.

Yes, I downloaded it again so I could track him. And he was nowhere near where she'd mentioned.

Listen...I hopped in my car and followed the app straight to him. By the time I arrived, it was about 7 p.m., so the sun was setting. I pulled in, searched the parking lot for his car, and boom! I found it! I mean this app was so on point it took me to the exact place where it pinpointed him. Yes, I was a hot mess. I parked about a hundred feet away. This was a massive apartment complex, so I was not sure exactly which apartment he was in. I sat in my car, and I watched his vehicle. I called him while I waited, and he did not pick up. I kept watching. A few minutes later, I saw people moving in the backseat of the car. Then a light came on. Someone was looking at their phone. I already knew what's up, but I kept watching. About twenty minutes later, he and a woman climbed from the backseat to the front. They sat for about ten minutes and then got out of the car. He walked her to the apartment. The apartment was far from where he was parked, so I got out and walked over to his car. I waited. I was calmer than I had ever been, but I refused to leave. I wanted to see the look on his face. It was cold outside, so I decided to get back in my car and move it closer. I now had a view of the apartment and of his car. Here I waited.

I called Danishia and told her what was going on.

"*Girl, why are you sitting there by yourself?*" she said.

"Listen, I am not leaving until I see him; otherwise he is going to lie. So I will sit right here all night if I need to."

Chileeee, the new me could never! I waited a long time. I spoke to my cousin for about three hours. Finally, he walked out to his car. Alone.

"Girl, let me call you back; he's getting in the car."

"*Call me back for real!*" she said.

Once he shut the door and started the ignition, I sat my seat up discreetly. He began to reverse out of the parking spot. I started my car and drove over to him, blocking him in as he was exiting the parking lot.

He saw me. He looked at me like a deer in headlights.

At first, I couldn't even open the car door. I was so frantic. After a couple tries, I unlocked the door, hopped out, and ran over to him.

As I opened the driver's door, he yelled, "Please don't mess up the car. Just please don't mess up the car!"

I don't know who I became in that moment, but I was filled with so much rage that I could not control myself. I started punching him right in his face until I ran out of strength. He couldn't do anything but hold his arms up to protect himself. I stopped, said nothing, walked back to the car, and drove off.

I know, I lost it. And I never, ever lose it. I'd never lost my composure in this way. This was not the plan. It was never the plan. And because I never planned for this, I didn't have a plan to get out of it. When I yelled, "I'm a good fucking woman" through my tears as I sat back in my car, it wasn't because I was trying to convince him of it. It was because I had to remind myself of *what and who* the fuck I was.

I went back to his mother's house. I grabbed everything I could fit in two plastic bags. I didn't know where I was going, but I KNEW that I was not staying here. The house was quiet; his mom and stepdad were upstairs. I am not one to draw attention, so I'd rather get what I think I need and get out. No words were exchanged between us. No eye contact was made. I was out of there in twenty minutes. He did not try to stop me, and I wasn't waiting for him to stop me. I never received an apology for that night. Even to this day, I have never received an apology.

Once you are privy to the truth the very first time, you don't need to ask for answers or ask anything for clarity. I'd already seen the truth multiple times with my own eyes; there wasn't anything to discuss here. I should have had this bravery two years prior to this. I actually wouldn't call it brave because I had more fear of staying than I did leaving. This moment was a result of me not taking myself seriously. This was comfortability within chaos. This was low self-esteem at its finest. When you continue to ask for details, what you are doing is asking questions in hopes they provide you with enough of an explanation for you to convince yourself to continue to deal with them. It is incredibly important we stop giving people multiple chances to play in our faces. I allowed it to happen in this relationship for four years. I stayed with him this long because of how he made me feel in the first nine months. If you know you need to leave them alone, you've already got all the evidence you need to make a decision. When a person continuously shows you that they're not for you and you continue to pursue them, they will hurt you until you have no choice but to leave. I ultimately played myself.

I spent a few nights at his aunt's house until I could figure out what I was going to do. She told me I could stay longer, but I didn't trust his family. I thanked her for her hospitality, and I kept it moving. I began staying at my office. I would sleep underneath my desk then head out to my car at around 4 a.m. when custodial came to clean. At around 6 a.m., I would head to the gym to work out and shower. I tried to remain as discreet as possible. I had no clue where I was going to go or how long I could hold out doing this. But I knew I wasn't going back.

Stacey,

It's okay if you don't know what to say or do right now. You are in unknown territory. You have never been here before, so it makes sense that you don't know exactly how to move. You are scared, but God never gave us the spirit of fear. Breathe, have faith in Him, and be patient with yourself. Your heart may be crushed, but it opened your eyes. Even when you feel broken you can re-build. Trust yourself enough to get back up. You will figure it out soon like you always do.

Anastasia

This was God's answer to that prayer in church. I felt guilty about a divorce, but I believe in my heart God moved suddenly so I could end that chapter before things got worse. I couldn't believe I got this response a mere eight hours later. I don't think I have ever gotten an answer to a prayer this fast. I was so angry at myself because I never thought a person could be like this. But this is exactly what I told myself I would do if it ever got this bad. I wasn't sure where I would go or how I would get there. Who had I become? I didn't know this woman in the mirror. I completely lost myself. I intended to live my best life, but I was living out my best lie. *Maybe God wants it to look hopeless. Maybe He's allowing the situation to seem impossible so I'll know it was Him when the breakthrough happens. Maybe this isn't the end, but perhaps, a new beginning. Maybe it was supposed to be a mess so the final result will be all the more sweet.*

My back was against the wall, but I was determined not to move back to Milwaukee—or back home, as many would have. I did not move to California for him, so I wasn't moving back because of him. The next few weeks, I would be tested with never-ending trials. It is amazing that God is so faithful to wreck your plans before they wreck you. Or in my case, potentially kill you. You can never save someone by allowing them to destroy you. You are deserving of full and unyielding love. You don't have to settle for anything less. You are still learning even when you lose your way. I can't be everything to everyone if I am nothing to myself. I walked away from my marriage to save Anastasia.

When will you get tired of being "okay" with things you're not okay with?

TRUTH JOURNAL

TRUTH JOURNAL

DEAR BEAUTIFUL WOMAN,

Endings don't require drama or toxic behaviors. You can end something because it's not what you want, it doesn't fit where you're going, you're tired of trying to make it work, your needs have changed, or you can no longer accept what is happening. You don't have to wait for a major offense to let things go. You don't have to fight until you have nothing left to give. It's okay to bow out gracefully. Sometimes peace is more important than giving someone a piece of your mind.

Anastasia

CHAPTER FIVE

THE MIRACLE AND THE MISTAKE ARE THE SAME THING

> "The Lord is close to the brokenhearted, and He saves those whose spirits have been crushed."
>
> — Psalms 34:18 New Century Version

THE REAL TRAGEDY is loving someone despite knowing they're not good for you and then letting them go believing you were never enough.

After I gave all of myself...After I sacrificed so much of my life...After I put him first.

He could not change. Truth is, I was overqualified. I was more than enough. I just didn't believe it, so I stayed longer than I should have. I didn't follow my intuition. Staying in the wrong relationship or marriage is one of the most exhausting and emotionally draining occurrences that you could ever experience. It kills you from the inside out.

Above anything in this world, always value your own dignity and self-worth. Never be afraid to lose anything that compromises that. Actually, *find peace* with losing anything that puts you in a position to compromise your self-respect.

I didn't have time to really think about what was going on. I was 2,000 miles away from home, and my mind was simply focused on survival. I didn't call anyone for a few days except my mom. I could tell she was worried. I would say that everything was going well, but she knew I was lying. When she asked about him, I would pretend he was sleeping or at work. Mamas know EVERYTHING. Don't ever think you can fool them. I didn't mean to cause her any worry, but in this moment, I was feeling too much shame to give her the honesty she deserved. I didn't want the thoughts and opinions of others to disturb my already broken spirit, so I continued to keep this to myself. After three weeks of sleeping in my car, I just so happened to speak to a former client of mine, Teri. I'd sold her a home nearly five months prior, and she became like an aunt to me. She suddenly found her way into my exploding world by accident and, unbeknownst to her, she would manage to assist me in finding my way. I gave her a slight glimpse of what was happening, and she insisted I stay with her until I found my own place.

Teri lived in Los Angeles, and the drive to and from work was exhausting. Seventy miles each way. Thankfully, because of my hours, I drove against rush hour traffic. Our relationship was new, so I truly did not want to be a burden to her and her family. I had no money, and I was not sure how I was going to find an apartment. In the interim, I continued to go to work as if nothing happened. As much as I wanted to move back to Milwaukee, I promised myself that was not an option. No, I had not heard from him. No calls, no texts, no apologies. I wasn't upset. He'd never fought for the relationship, so I would have been a fool to expect it. I needed money fast. I refused to ask my husband, and I couldn't tell my dad. That wasn't an option at that moment. My boss knew something was going on with me, and she made an attempt to have a one-on-one conversation. When I am frustrated, I am someone who pours into my work, and she noticed my change in demeanor. As easy as it is for me to hide anything, *this*, this was a heavy burden. I'm naturally very guarded, and if I tell you ANYTHING severely personal, consider yourself having a part of my heart. I didn't go into details, but I told her that I was having trouble at home. I tried to hold back tears as best as I could. She knew exactly what I was saying. She referred me to the cashier's office at work and recommended I take out a loan to help me with what I needed. So I did. I planned to use it toward a security deposit for an apartment.

I spent day and night searching for a place. My first option was to return to a previous rental community we'd lived in. I stopped by, viewed a unit, and completed an application. Even though my name was still in their system, I was denied, despite having no issues, complaints, and rent paid on time. My credit score had gotten so bad because of missed student loan payments, personal and business loans we had, and other unpaid debt that I had allowed to pile up while in this relationship. It was at this moment when I realized that I'd neglected my own needs to focus on what I thought was the "greater good" of the marriage. And there I was, the half of the union that was suffering.

I was officially homeless. I had never been in a situation like this. I could not believe this had become my life. I finally told my mom the truth. After about a week, she began asking too many questions. I could no longer think of new lies nor remember the old ones. Of course, she knew something was severely wrong. She figured I'd left him, but she had no idea what I was truly dealing with. She never knew about the shooting or us living with his mom. I even downplayed the apartment issue because, Lord knows, she would have been in complete panic finding out her only child didn't have a place to live. As long as I was safe, I was going to continue to hold out until things turned around.

After weeks of searching, I ended up finding a listing on Craigslist. I really didn't like the unit, but I needed something, and the rent was well within my budget. I believed that this apartment was mine. I called the landlord and met with him the next day. I prayed he would understand my story. I was really just in a bad situation. He accepted me. No increased deposit or anything. After about six weeks, I finally had a place! I was so relieved! I moved my things that weekend. I rented a U-Haul. I needed help putting my belongings in the truck, so I texted my husband. I remember picking up the U-Haul and feeling so awkward driving this big truck all alone. His brother and cousin were at the house, and they loaded everything I had. I know what you're thinking...no, he didn't help. My husband never asked me where I was living, didn't apologize, and we didn't even speak to one another when I was grabbing my things. He never made eye contact with me and acted as if I wasn't even there. His cousin questioned why he was acting so cold toward me for no reason. "Girl," he said, "I don't give a f* about her leaving." To hear him say that as I walked out the front door completely crushed me. But I couldn't cry. Not here, anyway. Even though I wanted to shout, I knew he wanted to get a rise out of me. I gathered the rest of my things and got back in the truck as if I was completely unfazed.

Could I have asked him for money? Yes. I didn't because I am a woman who would rather show you that I also don't need you. I'd traded in my respect for money and allowed myself to be manipulated with it in the past. I wouldn't have heard the end of it, and that I could not allow. He may have thought I was going to stay down, but baby, I knew better.

I also took our two dogs because I knew they would be better off with me. I was in an unfamiliar neighborhood alone, and taking care of them could give me a little distraction. It took me a full day to get everything into my apartment. I got all of my belongings out of storage by myself. For the first time in my life, I felt abandoned.

In the midst of my sorrow, I simply thanked God that it was over. I was incredibly happy to have a place of my own to live. It was a small, one-bedroom apartment—no bells and whistles, but I was determined to fill it with peace. Throughout this process, I did not shed a single tear. I didn't have time to. Sometimes when the trauma is so deep, you simply move through the motions, and you can't feel or remember anything. I didn't fully process what was truly happening because I didn't know what was going to happen. I just knew that I literally had to save myself. Once I got all of my belongings moved in, I lay on my bedroom floor next to my dogs and cried. All of my emotions erupted like a volcano. The adrenaline I had disappeared; I ran out of gas. I was so exhausted that I could not move. I curled up on my mattress, nearly drowning in tears for a full day.

I was severely drained. My pores were oozing four years of pain, betrayal, lies, confusion, depression, manipulation, low self-esteem, and guilt. Trying to hold myself together for four years in a miserable relationship and marriage required more mental and emotional stamina than you would ever think possible. See, in these types of relationships you have two options: You will either let go, preserving yourself and your feelings first, or be dragged until you have no choice but to let go. In the former, if you haven't fully developed your self-confidence, you may question your decision to leave over what could have been described as a "minor incident," something that could be worked through. Leaving after you've held on far too long is a bit different. You know you stayed past your check-out date; therefore, you are not interested in going back. But the tremendous amount of stupidity and embarrassment you feel will make any woman want to hide under a rock.

Stacey,

You are not stupid. You are hurt. You made a decision. I hope you find the courage to love every part of you— the parts that you have sheltered by your insecurities. The parts that are worthy of the light that you have raided with darkness for so long.

Anastasia

As I attempted to arrange my belongings in a five hundred square foot apartment, I thought to myself that this alone time was long overdue. If it wasn't forced, I would have never gotten to this place on my own. This was simply the turning point of my transformation and where the real work would begin. I had been in and out of relationships consistently since I was 16. Being alone, and in this way, was completely new to me. I didn't know how to be single. It didn't matter if the relationships were good, bad, or indifferent. I needed a sense of companionship. I had never been so insecure in my entire life. Why did I put up with so much? I could think of at least three times I should have left him, but instead I felt the need to mend something that was never even worth it. I changed myself and lost my identity for him. What was it about him? Who really was I? Why did I subconsciously believe that I deserved how I was being treated? These were questions I wanted answers to. I needed these answers so I could begin my healing process.

Settling is a byproduct of fear. We are created to desire companionship, and the thought of being alone for a long period of time can be intimidating. We've become co-dependent. We are accustomed to discounting our value so unworthy people can afford us. Stop putting so much trust in a man doing you right. Put that trust in yourself and do right by you. Trust yourself to move on when necessary instead of waiting, wishing, and hoping he will treat you better. Stop putting on shows and attempting to convince a man to see your value. People never appreciate valuable things that they aren't used to or have no experience with handling. There are times we are searching for signs and pleading for answers from God

> **We are accustomed to discounting our value so unworthy people can afford us.**

about certain situations that we never sought wisdom about from the beginning. Sometimes His silence is the "sign" we need. God has equipped us with the inherent ability to "feel" when something isn't right. He will send small clues and whispers that we tend to ignore. There is no need for a huge demonstration to tell you to end something or to walk away. You know deep down what you should do. Don't ignore that gut feeling or nagging within. That's the clarity you prayed for, not confusion.

> **The journey to discovering who you truly are often means confronting your past.**

Do Not Just Slay Your Weaknesses; Dissect Them and Figure Out What They Are Feeding On.

The journey to discovering who you truly are often means confronting your past. Have you ever thought to yourself, "Wow, I sound just like my mother!" or even caught yourself following the routine you watched her do for years? We are shaped by our parents, siblings, and our environment. One morning, I woke up and thought about my relationship with my father. I love my dad with everything in me, and I know he feels the same. He comes through for me with anything that I ask and has never failed to show up for me. But he is disconnected from his emotions. He wasn't the father who was mushy over his daughter. I was never "Daddy's Little Princess." As a child, I believed I needed to be on a quest to receive emotion from him.

As an adult, I understand that he may have never received the emotion he needed from his own parents. Sometimes people just can't give you what they didn't get. They simply don't know what it looks like, and it may feel completely awkward to them. In many of my relationships, I didn't let go of it or dissolve it when I needed to. There was a longing feeling inside of me. The need to want to prove myself—the same feeling I'd had as a child. If we often felt rejected in childhood, the feelings of rejection or abandonment can cause the feeling of "love" inside of us. Fighting for approval and acceptance has become a "normal" feeling of what love feels like.

Stacey,

Cutting ties with people who hurt you isn't enough. You must also cut ties with the version of yourself that allowed the treatment to happen.

Anastasia

I also grew up with a sense of intimidation by my father. He has grown softer and our relationship has grown over the years, but he was serious and isolated. Even though he never turned me down from my wants or needs, I always hesitated to ask him for anything. The person I was with my mom and the person I was with my dad were night and day. With my dad, I was quieter, more serious, and I mostly kept to myself. With my mom, I was my

> **Your actions in your relationship often reflect what you lacked in your childhood.**

authentic, annoying self. I realized I was also like this with men. How I viewed them, whether it was more like my mom or my dad, determined how I acted around them. I could be visiting my dad, and we could spend hours in separate rooms. Nothing was ever wrong; it was normal. With my mom, that was never the case. I remember riding in the car with my ex for about an hour. We didn't speak the entire ride. Not because we were upset; actually, there wasn't anything wrong although he may have thought I had an issue. That was just the way it was. It was awkward to him yet normal to me. This was a crucial awakening. I did not do well with men who showed their emotions and sensitivity. I always pushed them away or friend-zoned them. Although this was what I desired, it wasn't given from the first man in my life, so I pushed it away. Your actions in your relationship often reflect what you lacked in your childhood. It is said that women will mimic the relationship with their father in their romantic relationships. This can either be positive or negative. We develop an unconscious schema of what love is based on the way we were treated by the primary caregivers in our lives. As adults, we are typically attracted to people who behave toward us in the same manner. We don't always have relationship problems. Sometimes we have childhood problems that are disguising themselves as relationship problems. When we have an epiphany, we recognize our inner child's cries for help, and we define what a healthy version of companionship means for us. Then we can move away from our childhood patterns.

How many times have you said, "Oh, he's too nice" about a potential love interest then friend-zoned him? It is imperative to discover why you are the way you are. Dissecting yourself, indicating triggers, and recognizing patterns of bad behavior can help prevent you from falling into and break negative cycles. It is important to note that I cannot place any blame on my father as a grown woman who understands her actions. Yes, it has influenced me, but where I come from and what I have experienced will not become my crutch. You can leave a toxic relationship but if you don't heal what attracted you to them, you will meet them again. Same character traits, different person. I refuse to repeat a similar experience in each relationship. In my future, I know how to move accordingly with men. One thing I've learned is that our parents did the absolute best they could, and yet their choices can still wound us. Seeing unhealthy patterns in your family and deciding that those patterns end with you and will not be passed down to future generations is an extremely brave and powerful decision.

We all have weaknesses. Even the most honest, confident, organized, and compassionate types have them. The first step to identifying a weakness is to admit you have them. Some of us have chosen to remain blissfully ignorant of our shadows. There is a bubble of protection we've created in order to avoid direct confrontations with our fears and traumas that will be completely torn away. Dissect what your weaknesses are. Either you're going to make a choice to beat your demons, or they will eat you.

When you are interviewing for a job, the hiring manager often asks what your weaknesses are. I've always hated that question. Mainly because I knew I didn't have a good answer, nor could I be completely honest. My standard answer was always something generic like, "I don't ask for help when I should." My two weaknesses are that I am extremely hard on myself and somewhat of a perfectionist. I am definitely the type to handle everything on my own, and I don't share many details of my personal life because 1) I don't want to burden others, and 2) I have a fear of being judged. It is natural for me to keep everything to myself out of this fear, but I have learned that if you don't get it off your chest, you will never be able to exhale.

As a child, I didn't have much room for error. At least, in my opinion. I was always enrolled in some sort of extracurricular class, music lessons, or activity I wasn't particularly interested in. I know that my mom wanted the best for me and urged me to discover my talents. But I simply wanted to hang out with my friends. She would nag whenever I wanted to quit an extracurricular she'd signed me up for. So I grew up with the feeling that I had to constantly be doing or achieving something or I wasn't doing anything. In my adolescence and early adult years I took much criticism to heart and that caused me to become extremely hard on myself. After graduating college, I remember applying to many jobs and being denied. I never threw in the towel, but I felt defeated. I went into a depression because I believed that my hard work should have paid off. And for months it felt like it didn't.

I should have moved by now.
I should have a job by now.
I should be earning $XX by now.

I was caught up in a timeline of perfection for my life. Allowing things to "flow" was a concept that took years for me to grasp. In this season of my life, my pattern of thinking hindered my growth because it caused me to constantly proclaim my negatives rather than celebrating my positives.

When You Lower Your Standards, You Lose

Your steps are ordered, even when it hurts. You don't get do-overs in life because you don't need them. You needed to mess up. You had to make those mistakes. Your heart had to be broken. You needed to lose your way. There are lessons to be learned in those moments that could not have been delivered any other way. Trust your individual process. God can take away any misery, but if He takes it away, you will never learn the lesson. The pain won't leave until it finishes teaching you. If it hasn't left, it's not finished. Your willingness to experience discomfort might be one of the most useful skills you can develop. Everything in life worth doing, being, or having requires discomfort in one form or another. The process of adopting better habits or letting go of old ones are full of discomfort. Learn your lesson so you don't have to see it again.

Every time you lower your frequency to meet someone on their level, you will pay for it. It is extremely hard to pull someone up, yet very easy to be pulled down. It is so important to be equally yoked in any relationship, especially romantic ones. How you love yourself is how you teach others to treat you. For the most part, relationships are a reflection of where and who you are at any given period of time. The partner we select is often the external validation of what we are currently experiencing internally. Your relationship is not a fix-it-all situation. It will not repair your heart issues, your childhood abandonment issues, your love issues, your depression issues, your loneliness issues, or your low self-esteem issues. It exposes them. So if you spend your entire life with the mentality of, "My trauma damaged me, and that's why I am the way I am" instead of learning how to heal and grow from it, you are your biggest problem. Not your relationships. Stop making your traumas a scapegoat for your lack of accountability. Anything negative that happens to you throughout life was sent for you to destroy the pattern. Not become a victim to it.

As you become whole, the more likely it is that your relationships will reflect that transformation. We attract what we are, and as we change, so do our relationships. This doesn't mean that when you grow, you automatically have to say goodbye to your significant others or friendships. It does mean that in order to survive, any relationship you have will need to be able to grow with you. If the growth doesn't happen, you will become stuck and stagnant in your own transformation. This is the fork in the road. You will have to decide what you love more: the relationship or yourself.

Sometimes the Idea of Someone is Better Than the Reality of Them

The more I prayed for my marriage—for God to restore it, fix it, change it—the more it fell apart. I do not condone divorce by any means, but God does not put every marriage together. Sometimes people do. We let our emotions, insecurities, fears, and our timetable rush us into something that should have only been temporary. I believe there are too many people asking God to bless relationships that He was never a part of from the beginning. And many marriages God will save. I was never my husband's rib; that's why we both had difficulty breathing in our union. I was always anxious about something, and I didn't listen to my gut feeling before chaos infiltrated our relationship.

Stacey,

I'm sorry that you gave him everything you had without first making sure he was truly worth it. I know your heart hurts as you delve into your past mistakes, combing over every single detail. Why didn't you leave after the first lie? Why did you give up your apartment? Why couldn't you stop while you were ahead? Why didn't you listen to Danishia? Yeah, you knew better but still chose the opposite. Now you're dealing with feeling irrelevant, an unfortunate side of the consequence. Forgive yourself for the years you gave him. Forgive yourself for making multiple efforts without reciprocation. Forgive yourself for being young and dumb. Forgive yourself for hesitating to walk away. Forgive yourself for ignoring God's voice. Forgive yourself for making the wrong choices. Forgive yourself for loving in spite of betrayal. Forgive yourself for the pain you feel. Forgive yourself for not knowing what you didn't know until you lived through it. If your absence didn't motivate him, then your presence never would. Please understand what you think you lost couldn't stay anyway.

Anastasia

Choosing a partner is a very important decision that shouldn't be taken lightly. Your partner affects everything in your entire life: your mental health, your peace of mind, the love inside of you, your happiness, how you get through tragedies, your success, how your children will be raised, and so much more, so you must choose very wisely. This is serious business. No one wants to hear the term "business and marriage" in the same sentence, but it is the truth. It is a lifelong investment that will affect you even after you split. My divorce cost me more than I wanted to pay. Move cautiously and never settle. Although the best gift my ex-husband ever gave me was a new perspective. Because before him, my biggest fear was being alone. After him, my biggest fear is settling.

> **If you are looking for love, the fastest way to get it is to focus on your own love.**

Remember the Treasure Doesn't Do the Hunting

If you are looking for love, the fastest way to get it is to focus on your own love. Love of yourself, love of your dreams and goals, love of your passion, and most importantly love of God. When you embody love, love will inevitably find you. If you cannot be happy alone, you will not be happy in a relationship. If you cannot make money on your own, you will not be able to make money in a relationship. If you do not love yourself, then you will make it difficult for someone else to love you. If you don't know what makes you happy, no one else will either. If you cannot pray or connect with God on your own, then it will be impossible to have a spiritual and godly connection with a significant other.

First, build yourself up before you try to manifest a man or relationship. You will only attract your mirror image and someone who you can handle. If you are in pursuit of fulfilling your life's assignment, then God will lead you to someone who will be a part of fulfilling it. Feeling lonely, desperate, heartbroken, or incomplete without a partner will not attract them. It will actually repel them. If anything, it will cause you to attract the wrong kind of love like I did. That person will only intensify the pain you're already in. It is not spoken about enough, but there is a large amount of unlearning that needs to occur after you've had a bad man and before you experience a good one. Inner healing is required before you can enter into a loving relationship with another individual. I clung to patterns that

I recognized I needed to work on before I engaged in new love. I discovered self-doubt inhabited my spirit. I didn't dream like I used to, and as life knocked me down, I wasn't sure if I could reach my goals without a partner. I spoke negatively. I sabotaged myself and was truly my own worst enemy. Life and death are in the power of our tongues; therefore, your future lies in the words you speak. I shrank for the comfort of others, and I made sure to withhold my own light not to offend or intimidate someone else. I had a fear of vocalizing my worth, and I tried very hard not to be confrontational with anyone. I dislike arguing so I tended to suppress my feelings to be easy to get along with. I engaged in more than enough one-sided connections; they're draining. Yet instead of focusing on myself, I felt a sense of temporary fulfillment helping someone else in need even if they weren't reciprocating my energy. I also wasted a lot of time. I didn't value it, and in hindsight, it's the thing that frustrated me the most as I healed.

Being single can be the best thing to happen to your mental health. Spend that time addressing all the things you need to work on, as opposed to dwelling on past relationships or anticipating new ones. If you refuse to change, you can't expect to see change in your life. I became angry with me whenever I caught myself thinking about situations that triggered my insecurities or painful experiences. I made the choice to work through those provoking moments so I didn't carry them from person to person. I pray more women will learn how beneficial being alone for a season is. Take time off from dating, remaining celibate, discovering who you truly are, soul searching, figuring out what you want out of life, and learning

> **The moment I stopped settling was the moment I took back control of my life.**

to be content and happy with or without a relationship. The better you become, the more successful everything attached to you will be. Your healing and self-improvement should not fall last on your to-do list. Your life rises and falls on what you think and feel about yourself. Everything that you do or don't do stems from your thoughts.

The lie that we've been sold is that you need someone else to come into your world and make your life better with their love. External love is often fleeting and rarely unconditional. People give it and take it away, and you have no control over that. Focus on being great enough for you and build the kind of life you want to be living regardless of who is or isn't in it. The moment I stopped settling was the moment I took back control of my life. I couldn't keep lowering my worth just because he couldn't see it. I knew I had a lot to offer someone who was worthy of me, and that wasn't my ex. He didn't value me. He kept holding me down instead of lifting me up. He only appreciated having me around so he could mentally abuse me into believing I would never find anyone better than him. That no one else would be interested in me because I was divorced. He needed to hurt me in an attempt to feel better about his own insecurities. The longer he could keep lowering my self-esteem, I would never find the courage to choose myself. During our arguments, I found myself internalizing the hate he spewed my way, and I lived with shame prior to walking away. I knew I wasn't powerless or unsubstantial, *but was I?* When you love someone and want to build them up and they attempt to diminish you, you become uncertain of yourself. My sadness would eventually build a home inside of me. Once I decided sadness could not create a permanent resting place in my heart, I found just enough strength to pick myself up. When I said I would never allow anyone to belittle or manipulate me into believing I wasn't good enough, the tables turned. I knew I deserved better. Leaving him was the best decision I ever made.

Stacey,

You can love a person deeply and truly and still decide that doing so from a distance is best for your emotional and mental health. A lover doesn't discourage your growth, they inspire it. When you learn to love yourself, your taste in men will change.

Anastasia

I truly believe that every single person has to go through something that absolutely destroys them so they can figure out who they really are. We've all been through something we weren't sure we could get through, but we did, and it completely changed us at our core. Some of us are still going through this, but it's how we get through that determines our destiny.

Bad chapters still create great stories. Wrong paths can still lead to right places. Failed dreams can still create successful people. Sometimes it takes losing yourself to find yourself.

In order to love your authentic self, you cannot hate the experiences that shaped you.

TRUTH JOURNAL

TRUTH JOURNAL

Happy 28th Birthday, Stacey!

wheww chileee, you have been through quite a storm! But you made it out of the eye of the hurricane, and believe it or not, your world remains intact. You didn't have to move back home. You did find an apartment. It's just you and your doggies. It's not perfect, but you have everything you need at this moment. You have made it to the other side, and your divorce is almost final. The landscape is different. The lens has been adjusted. You have changed, too. You're not the same woman you were not so long ago.

It's time to rebuild your life. Right now, your heart hurts. You're embarrassed. You're upset you got yourself in this situation. You don't know if you can forgive yourself. Starting over will not be as bad as it seems. You have the opportunity to become exactly who you are destined to be. You will take every brick thrown at you...every lie, every rumor, and every setback to lay the foundation for your future. Eventually, you will revel in how strong and resilient you've become.

These next few years will show you who your true friends are. You will form stronger relationships with those that you already consider your best friends. And you will also see your share of fair-weather friends. Some will see your biggest downfall and find joy in the midst of your pain. Do not be saddened; not everyone has your best interest at heart. Instead, embrace those wonderful friendships that you have and invest more time in them. If you do that, you will be a much happier person. Your life will be more fulfilled.

In your late twenties and early thirties, your relationship with God will grow by leaps and bounds. So get ready to give yourself to Him. You will become much closer to Him, and it is heartache that will get you there. In this season, you will learn to trust Him in every circumstance. Nothing... not a single hurt, tear, or disappointment will be wasted.

What God has for you will always be for you. You will see what prayer, faith, and believing in God's timing will do for you. You will surrender to Him and He will grant your biggest, deepest desires.

Your life will not change until you get desperate for it. Until you get so desperate that you don't care who is looking. Until you get so desperate you don't care what you have to do to get connected to God's glory. You have all of these ideas and all of this creativity but haven't been desperate enough to manifest change in your life...until now.

You will take a huge leap of faith. You are not sure whether you will fail or soar, but you are ready for change and the challenges that come with it. When you have a breakthrough, you can't go back to playing small. Get ready for the pressure that comes along with being center stage.

FOOLISH FAITH

It will take time, but you will learn to give yourself more credit for what you overcame.

You didn't lose your mind.

You still believe in love.

You still believe in marriage.

You didn't fall into bitterness.

You have learned the power of forgiveness.

You have become gentle with yourself.

You own your past and who you are. Not many people can do that.

You stopped trying to conceal your scars. They have become your strength.

You learned not to be concerned with the thoughts and opinions of others.

You are fearlessly transparent; that is your superpower.

You understand the power you possess today directly correlates to the pain you've experienced.

Your life is nothing you ever wanted, but everything you've ever needed. You've made medicine from your pain. You're that kind of warrior. One day you will thank God for this beautifully broken season. Life tried to crush you. Instead, it made you a diamond. Everything you have gone through has set you up for everything you've asked God for.

You are living proof that you can walk through hell and still be an angel.

With Love,
Anastasia

CHAPTER SIX

SOMETIMES GOD WILL ANSWER YOUR PRAYER, YET YOUR SITUATION WON'T CHANGE. BUT SOMETHING EVEN BETTER WILL. YOU.

> "When troubles come your way, consider it an opportunity for great joy. For you know that when your faith is tested, your endurance has a chance to grow. So let it grow, for when your endurance is fully developed, you will be perfect and complete, needing nothing."
>
> — James 1:2-4 New Living Translation

TROUBLES ARE OFTEN blessings in disguise. The more we can test our limits and capabilities, the more we will learn about ourselves. We want to grow within our comfort zones, but that is impossible. Most of us won't feel joy or see the growth of a setback or failure. However, you can't skip chapters. That's not how life works. You have to read every line and meet every character. You won't enjoy all of it, and some chapters will make you heartbroken for weeks. You will read things that will make you cry, and you will have moments when you don't want the pages to end. But you must keep going. Stories keep the world turning.

What they don't tell you is that the healing hurts more than the wound. God answered my prayer, I spent a few weeks in disarray, but I was able to move and begin a new chapter on my own. I believed I would still have forward momentum, yet I was still stuck. I prayed for an answer, and I received it. I moved on it. I followed through, yet I was still HERE. Emotionally, I was empty. I was relieved, but still drained. I was expecting a different result once I'd gotten settled into my apartment. I thought when I stepped out on faith, I would continue to see wins unfold in my life. At least, that is what we are taught. That when we trust God and make a move first, He will do what we cannot do. What we don't discuss is how much work needs to be done on our part, and that stepping out on faith is JUST the beginning. Sometimes following your heart means losing your mind. So yes, chill. This is part of the journey.

In the midst of your transformation, you might feel like everything is falling apart, but in reality, everything is coming together. Maybe you have followed your heart into something, and it didn't work out as you expected. Does that mean you still made the wrong choice? Not necessarily. Consider that you are planted exactly where God intended for you to be in order to grow your faith. Many people are actually afraid to heal because their entire identity is centered around the trauma they've experienced. They have no idea who they are outside of their pain, and the unknown can be terrifying. Suffering is easy. If we so choose, we can all find numerous things to be sad about. I spent a very long time being embarrassed. I dealt with the pain for so long that it caused me to view myself through the lens of the treatment I accepted. The trauma defined our relationship and became part of my identity. I became embarrassed of myself. He was gone, but the mentality I'd developed lingered. We tend to stay in things we think or believe we deserve. And even when the presence is gone, we must work on our mind to eliminate the false narrative. I expected to just feel better. I thought a new job, more money, new friends, even a new man would make me feel so much better, but in this season, I needed to completely rely on myself. I was forced to develop an entirely new relationship with me.

 I was okay with being single, but I wasn't okay with being still. I needed progression. I needed to feel like I was moving forward and getting myself out of the hole I'd gotten stuck in. I tried connecting with old friends, yet they had their own lives and their own personal storms. I went on several job interviews that went so well I believed I would be offered a position, only to never receive an offer. I didn't have any money to shop or travel my way into some sort of temporary happiness. I joined dating apps, and the only guys who contacted me were people I had absolutely no interest in. I even went on two dates that went way south, and I gave up dating apps altogether! I needed something to distract me from the consequences of my own choices. I wanted the discomfort to go away. When we are in situations that are troubling, we distract and satiate ourselves in an effort to alleviate the pain. We quickly fill the gaps and move on to the next source of pleasure. We continue our chasing because silence is scary. Real growth begins when you are tired of your own ish! When there's no noise, we are forced to face ourselves and everything we've internally neglected. In that quiet moment, we make our uncomfortable realizations.

Don't Let the Process Punk You Out of the Promise

God is not Santa Claus. God is not a genie. He will bless you on His time, but you must move your feet first. When you have been bound for some time, it becomes your normal, and freedom becomes work. I sat in a season of nothing, broken and naked before God, so He could force me into doing the work. Otherwise, I would have never moved! If you have been battling depression for a long time, that is your normal. If you have struggled a long time, that is also your normal. If you have been broke for a long time, all you know is having barely enough. Whatever your chain is, make this your year to do the work to break it. When I got serious in following God's request for me to write *Foolish Faith,* I was determined because I don't have another year to stay on the same level I was on.

God will frustrate your process to reorder your priorities. I wanted God to bless me first, then I would do the work later. Oh no, baby. We feel that things are just going to happen, and yes, some things God will do, but many things we have to do first. And what God asks you to do most times won't be easy.

> **God will frustrate your process to reorder your priorities.**

Often, it is to break the culture from which you were built, to create a new standard of living. Generational curses go beyond poverty. It's staying in bad marriages, it's having your path dictated for you, it's being abandoned or rejected for standing in who you are, it's not believing in yourself or your dreams, it's settling for whatever you can get, it's not knowing you are worthy or valued, it's women being unprotected, it's men not being accountable. Lack of money or resources is included but there's still so much more that needs to be broken. This will not be just for you, but for generations to come. People think being blessed is easy. In all honesty, being blessed is harder than not being blessed. To whom much is given much is required. That is REAL. Nothing God does is just for you, and when you have a calling on your life, everything must start over and move according to His way and will.

It was extremely important for me as a woman to learn how to build a life of my own. I wanted this period of growth to be separate from any man. Separate from what I have grown accustomed to within myself. We generally don't want to do what it takes to walk into our blessings. It doesn't line up with our desires, but we will not be arbitrarily blessed just because we want it. You must give up who you used to be to become who God has called you to be. I had to deprogram myself of everything I thought about myself up until I was twenty-eight years old. I settled too low. I settled for what people said. I settled for old beliefs. I settled for generational curses. I settled for old criticisms. I settled for old emotions. I settled for what was easy. The level that you settle on is the level that you see yourself. For years, I waited on God, and I never saw Him move on the things I prayed for. I waited and waited, and I fell into such disappointment in God that my faith became challenged. After over two years of becoming frustrated with myself and God, I realized I couldn't avoid my own confrontation with my mindset any longer. I tried to complain my way out, but that didn't work. I was so uncomfortable. I began going to therapy. I needed to heal. Not only from what my ex did, but also from breaking my own heart. You can seek counseling as often or as little as you would like. *There is absolutely nothing wrong with therapy at any age.* I went for a specific reason while I was married. Now that I was trying to navigate this new world of mine, my reasons are completely different. I was asked to discuss each significant relationship from my past. We talked about why it ended, why did I choose them, why did I stay after various incidents. What was it about their character that reminded me of my childhood—positive or negative—to uncover patterns that stuck with me? What was I ashamed of? What was I afraid of? Who had I done wrong? What guilt had found its way into my heart? How were all of these things causing me to hold myself back? Looking at yourself in the mirror and uncovering all the reasons why you are who you are is incredibly uncomfortable, which is why most people don't do it. Healing is not magical and pretty. It is exhausting and draining. It will break you down and remove the sense of pride that we all carry that holds us together.

Stacey,

Don't let the reality of what you prayed for scare you away from what you prayed for. Don't let that go over your head.

Anastasia

Reprogramming your unconscious thinking will take a lot of intentional effort on our part. Healing is done in layers. You have to spiral through these same emotional experiences until there is no energetic charge left to trigger you. Be patient with God and yourself. When you don't know what to do next, it is okay to sit still. Your mindset—a strong and positive one—is essential to developing healthy self-esteem. It is an important tool that affects our daily self-dialogue and reinforces our most intimate beliefs, attitudes, and feelings about ourselves. It could be possible that the work you're doing is not the work that God is intending for your growth. In order to progress, you must get into alignment. We get so caught up in what others are doing and how they recovered from their trials, but God uses our shortcomings in a way specific to the calling He placed over our lives. Don't make a single move out of fear, desperation, or anxiety to bypass this phase.

Things that began to shift in my discomfort:

- Abandoning control over uncertainty and accepting the unknown
- Appreciating what I had taken for granted
- Releasing and removing the need for perfection and pleasing others
- Shedding or holding tight to connections, relationships, and bonds
- Trusting and believing in myself

- Respecting and loving my body and myself
- Bringing light to the parts of myself I am ashamed of

When you heal yourself, you are also healing your mother, daughter, and every woman around you. Even if you have a moment of regression to a past habit or cycle, understand that it is normal. When I thought I was moving forward, a negative thought or situation would provoke my emotions and cause me to stumble backward. Growth is not one long continuous upward movement. You will attempt to return to previous versions of yourself along the way, and that's okay. The past is not too far behind, and we love familiarity. Give yourself the grace you need to accept that you won't get it right on the first try. The more you judge yourself and overthink the mistake, the harder it is to create a new state of mind out of each moment. Even if you don't like what you are experiencing, the point is to keep moving.

The disappointment I had kept me in this season longer than I needed to be. I wanted to live in an old version of myself that no longer existed. I wanted to be angry. I wanted to be petty. I wanted to curse people out. I wanted to have fun in the fast lane with multiple men. I wanted to be spiteful. I wanted to get revenge. All of that is easy because it is what you are accustomed to doing. Easy is what we naturally want to resort back to. In your transformation, the absolute biggest difficulty is when you are between two versions of yourself. When we can't yet reach what we want to see, we want to revert back to what we know. Returning obliviates all the work you have done thus far. Stretching can be painful. But the truth is, once you step up to your next level, you MUST leave your current level and everything associated with it.

Self-Work Is the Most Rewarding Project You Will Ever Complete

God isn't changing your circumstance because He's changing YOU within the circumstance. Your character, your inner strength, your integrity matters to Him more than the material manifestation of the things we pray for. The wisdom, the strength, and the maturity that grows within you are all things you need to sustain the calling God has on your life. This is the purpose within your pain.

I was prone to self-effacing and running away from myself. When I could not find another outlet, I was forced to do the inner work I'd avoided for many years. What does inner work look like? It looks like stripping down to your innermost core without the accolades, achievements, fashion, children, or partner and acknowledging who you truly are at your core.

It's about freeing ourselves from old programming, limiting beliefs, and empty attachments.

Break free of limiting beliefs. Your expectations create your reality. Unfortunately, it can mean that we're selling ourselves short without even noticing it. It's easy to allow yourself to fall short because then you aren't responsible for achieving something awesome. It's easy to settle in a failing relationship than to thrive in a great one. When have you truly ever held yourself fully accountable? Accountability is difficult because it raises the bar. When you lack this important trait and things don't happen or don't work out, there wasn't much to be upset about anyway. Greatness takes work. Greatness takes patience. Greatness won't just accept you for who you are. I have sold myself short many times—in friendships, relationships, my marriage, even my job. That saying *Pray for the best but expect the worst*? No! You pray for the best and walk in anticipation that something great is coming to fruition. It may not be today, but it is coming. End of story. **Bottom line: if you don't believe in it, it's never going to happen.**

Discover your "why." Without knowing your "why," you're in danger of living unconsciously. Figuring out your "why" in life is just as important as breathing. You can be, do, and have anything you want, but it's important to figure out where your desires come from. If you're looking to fill a deep void inside of you, you'll one day be surprised to discover that no matter how much money you make, recognition you receive, or goals you surpass, the gaping hole is still there.

Motivations that are based on competition, getting even, or validation do not ultimately serve you. Ultimately, you're taking someone else's opinion of your life more seriously than your own! You're giving your own power away without realizing it. But when you find inner clarity, those distinctions become clear. You'll be able to see what's real and what isn't.

Changing your old habits. Habits, whether "good" or "bad," are a form of unconscious behavior, and that's exactly why they're so difficult to change. We do these things without even thinking. Can you imagine that you could be spiritually and emotionally killing yourself without even knowing it? This is *that* important. Those habits become part of our autopilot. Use self-improvement techniques such as practicing gratitude, exercise, healthy eating, meditation, prayer, and positive consistent self-talk to give yourself upward momentum. Changing your habits is necessary because those types of deeply ingrained behaviors are not easy to shift. They've become embedded into the very fabric of our daily life.

Find true self-acceptance. Self-love is the magical missing tonic for so many people in the world. In general, we're not taught to love ourselves. Many of us are taught that our imperfections are avoidable, unacceptable, and unworthy of love. We stretch ourselves to try to meet an invisible yardstick of perfection (I'm a Virgo) that we all inevitably miss.

Media programming reinforces this idea. The aim of many marketing campaigns is to make us feel inadequate, thus giving us a reason to need something (a product or service) to make us truly happy. **The most important** self-work is learning how to truly love ourselves, freeing us from the shackles of external validation.

Getting down to your core requires facing some harsh truths. Unless you fall into a space where you are forced, coming face to face with the woman in the mirror is a daunting task. It is not easy to accept that I am the sole reason why I am where I am. I can't even blame my ex. Yes, he asked me to marry him, but I accepted the proposal knowing in my gut it was the wrong move. I was free to leave at any time. As women, we overlook the fact that no man keeps us hostage. I was in control then, and I am still in control now. We are always in control. When someone behaves in a way that you do not like, you are free to leave. Mentally, we trap ourselves in the idea of what we believe the relationship could look like. If you show a man that you'll stay with him through anything, he will keep putting you through everything. Loyalty is not how much pain you can tolerate from a man. We get so caught up in not betraying our men that we fail to realize the real betrayal is forgetting ourselves.

> **We get so caught up in not betraying our men that we fail to realize the real betrayal is forgetting ourselves.**

When we avoid this chapter in our lives, we run into the same situation over and over again. What you don't heal in your singleness will spread like a disease in your relationship. After my separation, God forced me to face this part of my life. Nothing moved until I drank the bitter cup of self-reflection. Every remnant of who I used to be was forced to be removed in this season.

The way we deal with pain teaches us about who we really are, who we love, and how we love others and ourselves. I came to understand that who I am is nothing but my reflection of my journey within myself. This journey has helped me realize that the more life unfolds, the more my spirit evolves together. It taught me to be humble and patient. It redefined the concept of perseverance, devotion, and enthusiasm. More than anything, it taught me what I needed to learn about compassion toward others, and most importantly the woman in the mirror.

Heartbreak made me love myself more. I don't think I would've ever discovered self-love without it. It was my own love that healed me after the heartbreak. Singleness restored the confidence that my past unhealthy relationships tried to strip me of. Whoever has to leave your life, let them leave, but don't you dare let them take your confidence with them when they go. I became a better woman than I was when I entered those relationships. Although it shouldn't have gotten to marriage, it was used to teach me some harsh lessons about myself. It was ultimately for my good.

FOOLISH FAITH

Life will teach you a myriad of things, and one of those is that you will lose and gain people all throughout your life. You will mature to a point where you accept the fact that certain people will only be in your life for that season, and that's okay. Some people are there to push you out of your comfort zone and open you up to the idea of a committed relationship. Others are to show you exactly what you don't want. When that season is up, you leave. I did not have this level of wisdom to know when to close a chapter. I decided to stick around for my feelings, potential, and the time invested. In actuality, that was the ticking time bomb. Release those relationships that disturb your peace. I've seen too many women, including myself, lose their senses while waiting for a man to come to his. Women become comfortable with what is killing them emotionally. No one likes being uncomfortable. You may not want to be alone. I get it, but how is being in pain a better option? How is being in the same situation year after year treating you? If it suits your best interest, it's okay to make a shift. It's okay to change directions. It's okay to outgrow the life you thought you wanted. When you feel like you are not good enough, you will chase after men who will treat you like you are not good enough.

The Fears We Don't Face Become Our Limits.

Stacey,

Can we have a moment of transparency here?

It's been a long time coming for you to have the courage to look at yourself in the mirror and take full accountability for not being where you wished you would be in your life by now. You've never been one to point fingers at others, but you also spent way more time feeling frustrated or sorry for yourself than you should have. You sulked in your own disappointments that you're solely responsible for. You have to stop driving yourself crazy to understand why something happened, and just trust that whatever happened is what your soul needed to grow from.

Anastasia

The wounds we want to heal in others, even in our relationships, often reflect the wounds we want to heal in ourselves. You will have a very hard time building new relationships, not just romantic ones, if you don't bring light and understanding to what has caused you pain, and the person you have become because of it.

Early in my healing, whenever I would talk to someone, I found myself having the desire to control them or not being able to receive support from them. Because there was a lack of safety, stability, support, and connection within my marriage, I subconsciously wanted to overfunction and do "all the work." I became extremely independent as a means of protection. I didn't want to compromise, and I expected a man to live within my bubble of comfortability. It was my way or the highway, and I was okay with that. I put my own needs above someone else's simply because I was afraid to navigate the terrain of my trauma. It was difficult for me to accept any assistance—no matter how great or small—because I can do it all myself. I was used to doing it anyway. The inability to receive support from others is a trauma response. This conditioning is a survival tactic. I did it to shield my heart from any type of disappointment, lies, or betrayals. You would not catch me depending on anybody, and ultimately I pushed people away. I believed that if I didn't put myself in a situation where I relied on someone, I won't have to be disappointed when they didn't show up for me, when they dropped the ball, or when they betrayed my trust...because people will inevitably hurt you, right? Wrong. People are not perfect, and yes, people will disappoint you just as you will disappoint others; we cannot avoid this. Extreme independence, however, is a trust issue. This lack of trust we have in others reflects the lack of trust we have in ourselves. Because we have made one poor decision, we think that we can't make good ones. We vow to never be in that situation again. Or we will control a situation in an effort not to make a bad one. But no matter how we dress it up and display it proudly to make it seem like this level of independence is what we've always wanted to be, the truth is we're wounded, scarred, and broken-hearted behind a protective brick wall. You are impenetrable. No hurt gets in. But no love gets in either.

Trusting yourself is directly related to your core self-worth. If we do not have a strong relationship with ourselves, we struggle to navigate our pain. In order to trust ourselves again, we must become vulnerable. Vulnerability means sharing yourself, honestly and openly. To combat the fear of vulnerability, you must first learn to love and accept your whole, authentic self. Loving ourselves is one of the toughest lessons we will ever face. We all have flaws, imperfections, embarrassing stories, and past mistakes we would love to forget.

Vulnerability involves letting the emotional walls of anger down to expose the more raw feelings of pain and love. In the past I would say, "I don't care" when describing a need, or when my feelings were hurt and I wanted to hide my true feelings. Sometimes it's easier to say we don't care because we don't want to risk the vulnerability that caring really causes. Stop saying you don't care when you do, or one day you won't care when you need to. Being vulnerable does mean exposing yourself to the potential for hurt and rejection. At the same time, risking vulnerability is also opening the door to the kind of relationship you truly long for—one built on authenticity, trust, emotional intimacy, and a deep connection. Loving yourself fully means committing to do the scary things that will improve your life.

When you allow someone new into your life, make sure you are not charging them for crimes from your past that they didn't commit. Many people won't get to experience true intimacy in their relationships because they refuse to push through their insecurity. To get to real intimacy, you have to go through insecurity. You will need to open up to share how you desire to be treated and still allow them the space to respond to your needs. Begin each new relationship with a level of optimism. You cannot manipulate or control the situation in an effort to keep them from failing you. It honestly doesn't work, it says more about you than them, you will be emotionally drained, and it prevents you from seeing who they truly are. I always say, allow people the space to do what they want to do, so you can see what they would rather do. It's that simple. What I am not implying is to allow yourself to be uncomfortable all in the name of making the person you are dating comfortable. Have the courage to speak up. Most people are not mind readers. Two things will happen: you'll either get what you need or realize that the source you are asking doesn't have the capacity to deliver. Both are gifts.

When you are ready, begin to open up slowly and allow yourself to be seen. You can begin with sharing small pieces of yourself. You don't have to tell your story all at once. If someone is interested in knowing who you are, it's worth taking the chance and being vulnerable. Push yourself to share what you can and express your feelings as well as you're able to. Someone who cares about you will want to know what has hurt you in the past, and they'll be patient enough to wait for the story you have to share. You are worthy of love, support, and partnership. And you don't have to bargain for it.

Once You Realize You Deserve the Best, Losing People Won't Even Matter

Don't constantly be the person who has to wait for the other person to decide if it's going somewhere or not. You can decide. It's YOUR time, YOU decide where things are going. Take some time to understand God's intention for relationships and marriage and what that means for you. My discontentment and burning desire to be in a relationship is no longer alive. That is not to say that I have no desire for a relationship and marriage. It just means that I am content. And as each birthday and holiday passes, I am at peace with knowing I am not accepting lavish gifts in exchange for the faulty behavior I have accepted. I sleep peacefully at night. My edges are intact. I am really excited to see the woman I will become, by myself, for now. The husband will come in due time. Truthfully, I don't want any type of husband—I had one of those before. And when I think about my dream life, I know that it requires patience, and I've got more work to do.

It is okay to be great by yourself. Sometimes being alone is an upgrade. It has a power that not many can handle. Focus on bringing the goals you've whispered to yourself for years to fruition. Discover God's purpose for your life. Use this season to start building that empire you always dreamed about. When the right man finds you, you will make each other better and develop a partnership. I love Anastasia enough to be left alone with just Anastasia. Not having a boo or anyone to text or flirt with is not a form of punishment to me any longer. The longer you have to wait for something, the more you will value it when it arrives. Because you aren't desperate for it, it will mirror what you truly deserve. Once we understand this and can love ourselves enough to be a solo act, we won't be desperate to be with anyone again. I will tell you from experience—it is so much worse to be in a relationship outside of God's will for your life. In order to truly hear God's voice, we need to let go of all of our distractions.

Being single for a season does not mean God is punishing you. In this season God may be:

- Protecting you
- Preparing you
- Loving you so much that He doesn't want you to settle for less than His best
- Loving you so much to help you work on yourself

A lot of my self-criticism came from a place of low self-esteem and high self-doubt. When you know what you want, you will have the focus to stay on track and keep working toward your goals. You must have a strong sense of self-belief and reassurance because you trust in your capabilities and growth potential. Be selective and intentional with the people you allow in your space. Every interaction is not beneficial. You don't find healing from an ex by stalking their social media or hating them with someone new. You will receive your healing from God's presence. I pray that you will recognize that God is the only one who can fulfill you. Focus on your purpose and what He has for you. Let Him be enough.

Those years of pain and struggles were necessary for you to learn and apply the lessons that allowed you to become your best self now. It wasn't time wasted; it was time invested. It resulted in you deciding to change your life for the better. It led to the realization that you needed to change, and it gave you the courage and determination to take action. It was a valuable exchange in order for you to not 'waste' the rest of your life. There is nothing wrong with wishing you'd changed sooner. The fact you're changing now is still something to be proud of.

I promise you, if you do the work, there will come a day that you will look up and be exactly the woman you thought you could be. The whispers of fear, mistakes, and insecurities disappeared when I learned there's beauty in embracing my past. With determination and courage, I breathed in the possibilities of the present and allowed myself to evolve. When I didn't allow a temporary circumstance to change me permanently, I became a force to be reckoned with. Your deepest emotional wounds will become your greatest superpowers once healed. There is a woman on the other side of this struggle that you are trying to become. This version of you will not come cheap, and it will require more than you've got. But it will come.

Don't settle in the transition...there's more.

TRUTH JOURNAL

TRUTH JOURNAL

CHAPTER SEVEN

BOUNDARIES; YOUR VALUES IN ACTION

> *"I have refined you, but not as silver is refined. Rather, I have refined you in the furnace of suffering."*
>
> — Isaiah 48:10 New Living Translation

YOUR TRUEST TEST of a woman is your level of self-care.
What's self-care? Self-respect.
What's self-respect? Self-love.
What's self-love? Self-preservation.
What's self-preservation?
Boundaries.

There is nothing more you can tell a woman who has had enough. I have grown into a woman who can walk away from what does not serve her. It didn't become that way until I had a long overdue conversation with myself about the boundaries I've enforced in my relationships, or lack thereof.

As a woman, there is nothing more disheartening, stomach turning, or attitude changing than a man that is not of his word. "Let's try to make it work for the third time because I love you." How many more years are you going to waste pretending ginger ale is champagne? It doesn't matter how much you hate getting to know new people; wasting time on someone who already has let you down is foolish. People hang on to relationships that died months or years ago as if it is just a phase. Nah!

Develop some boundaries; you're wasting time because you have become too comfortable. Familiarity will keep you stuck in pitiful circumstances, but because they're predictable, we stay in them until something painful calls us out. I've made many excuses for why people did the things that they did, and why it was okay for me to give them a second, third, or fourth chance to remain in my life. I did this out of guilt and out of fear. I'd pour from an empty cup for each person I loved, only to be left wondering why I never had anything left for myself.

We are trained and programmed to believe a lot of things, but one of the things we are not usually taught...correctly... is self-love. How can I find a million ways to love someone else, but somehow, I struggle with finding a dozen ways to love myself? I want you to aspire to have a heart so full that you are able to thoroughly love you and still love someone else without compromising you.

FOOLISH FAITH

Stacey,

I forgive you for settling when you were uncertain of your power. You've got a new story to write, and it looks nothing like your past.

Anastasia

I know there were a few people and experiences that contributed to your low self-esteem. I know that through these experiences you kept meeting more and more of the same heartaches because you didn't know you deserved better. You didn't know what this better should, could, or would be. I pray that with every ounce of your being, you will fight for your right to love yourself. One day, you'll love yourself fully, speak up clearly, you will feel confident, you will stand up straight, you will wear what you want, you will learn to say "NO," and you won't take shit from anyone anymore. One day, you will be able to see clearly what *better* looks like. And you will be able to smile because everything and everyone in your life is better for you because of the changes you made.

We live in a generation of "situationships," where being single, divorced, or widowed can be daunting, but it's incredible how those who refuse to settle get more than they asked for. Waiting is scary as it requires us to have faith and believe in an outcome that hasn't happened yet. It's even more difficult when those who have settled tell you that you are "asking for too much." The temptation to casually date due to loneliness is real. You need strength and prayer because the wait will cause you to lose hope. It's a fact that we are impatient. We don't even like to wait for our food, so when waiting for the right love to find us—*and I do mean find us*—we seek whatever is good for the moment. We want to act, to figure it out, and to know with certainty what's going to happen. To leave anything up to chance is simply beyond our level of comprehension because it immediately makes us feel insecure. We force situations we were never meant to be in to feel like something is moving—even if it's moving in the wrong direction.

Do you know how you gain self-love, high self-esteem, and confidence? By leaving toxic situations that weigh you down and cause you to feel bad about yourself. You've grown so accustomed to your low expectations that you don't see how those relationships are affecting how you feel about yourself. It's time to take your power back and be intentional about what you allow into your life. Anything you desire, positive or negative, is making its way to you at this very moment. The law of attraction is powerful. Once you establish yourself as powerful, confident, or strong, even business oriented, like-minded people will flock your way out of nowhere. And it's just God reminding you that when you can see something beautiful in yourself, others can see it and admire it as well. Imagine falling in love with your joy, your happiness, and your sanity before falling in love with anyone else.

After going through trauma, learning to pick yourself up is such an important thing that no one ever teaches you. You can transform your entire life by deciding what you're available for and creating boundaries to support that vision. My growth comes with no apology letter attached to it. It comes with no honey-coated words and actions. It comes with no guilt or regret. I'm grateful for anyone I was forced to leave behind because their absence helped me find more of myself.

When you have never been treated well, walking away from a toxic situation is an act of defiant faith. I know that access to my energy is a privilege. I am not afraid of my future. Nothing can fold me. I allowed my struggle to make me a better individual. We must stop allowing our struggles to make us weak individuals. Stop allowing it to make you pitiful. Stop allowing it to make you pathetic. You must look at your struggle as a fight. And I'm not leaving the ring without the belt. I knew that I had reached an ultimate level of self-respect when I stopped trying to convince a man to love me properly. Sometimes the best thing a person can do for you is to not choose you. Not being chosen puts us on the path that we're meant to be on. That heartbreak saved you. It was never supposed to work, and you would have just kept on trying. Stop allowing these men to be able to save you for later. We live in a culture where we celebrate women who endure toxic relationships instead of celebrating the women who have realized enough is enough. We need to stop teaching people that love is hard and complicated. *Toxic* love is hard and complicated.

The healing process is not easy. You feel alone and like no one understands what you are going through. You are mourning the loss of a significant part of your life. Every day is a challenge. A broken heart is one of life's mysteries. There is no immediate cure, and only time and inner work will give you the grace to truly rebound. It's something most will experience at some point in their life, but it does not last forever. You will find yourself smiling more and enjoying life again, but you must stay strong through the storm. Stop looking for closure. It's not necessary. You received closure once they treated you with disrespect. Stop entertaining your pain, and you will heal. Do not add difficulty to the process. It can cause you to carry a broken heart for years.

Don't stay updated on people who hurt you without remorse. You don't need to know how they are doing. You will never get over them if you keep watching their every move, so stop! Stop listening to people when they try to tell you about them, stop hanging out with their family, stop replaying the relationship over and over in your head. There's nothing more you could have done. And stay off their social media pages! Stop being faithful to a man that's no longer yours. I know, it sounds crazy. I've done it, and I know others have, too. By constantly checking his Facebook, keeping up with his every move, I stayed faithful to him. I wasn't particularly hopeful that things would work. I was loyal to my own foolish behavior and wasn't focused on my own life and healing. Keeping communication lines open leaves room for unwarranted behavior. You will start to question your decision to leave the relationship. It blocks the flow of positive energy you need to move you into your next phase. If you have children with a man, I understand this is not entirely feasible. However, limit your level of interaction and conversations to only concerns of your child(ren).

Stop thinking it will work out if you get back together; it won't. If they were the right one, they would have shown themselves to be so in the time you gave them. Returning to someone after they've shown you that they can't respect your boundaries is showing them that you don't respect your boundaries either. No, you didn't lose just because you are still single and they are dating. We tend to turn a breakup into a competition. Whether they are happy or not is none of your business. Just because they had better chemistry doesn't mean she's a better woman than you. She may be better *for him,* but you're better for someone else. Some choose apples over oranges. That doesn't mean oranges aren't good. It just means they wanted the apple. And if they're truly happy, that's amazing. And you know why? Because your turn to win is coming next. *No relationship is worth it if you are not happy.* You have already cried, prayed, and lost sleep. Your destiny is never tied to someone who left. If you made it before them, you can make it without them.

Stacey,

You can't make someone love you by giving them more of what they already don't appreciate.

Anastasia

It's hard to set boundaries when you don't know your worth. However, *knowing* your worth is still not enough. There are a lot of people who know they are worth so much more than what they put up with but haven't put their worth into action. There's knowing you deserve more versus refusing to settle for less. You can say you deserve better all you want, but if you continue to accept less than the best, you will always get mediocrity out of your dating life. You will stop settling for mediocre men once you start showing up in your own life as a confident, whole woman. Nothing changed in my life until I actually put some action behind it. When you decide to implement boundaries, you will discover what that actually truly means. You will need to decide what offenses are non-negotiables and which ones are worth second chances. How many times does a person need to show you they do not care about your feelings? How many times are you able to look beyond his poor character? How many times are they allowed to ghost or gaslight you? How many times will you stay after he cheats? How many lies do you need to hear? How long will you date someone that you don't trust? How many times does someone need to let you down before you realize they're not acting out of character? That IS their character. Once those boundaries are crossed, you will need to stand on them and move on. It may appear harsh, but people respect those who respect themselves, and even more so, a person who cannot be disrespected for a second time.

Boundaries for me meant more than a few days and nights alone. It meant having a dry phone. There was no one to surprise me on my birthday. I watched others get into new relationships and marriages. I dismissed men that weren't for me even though I wanted company. I wondered if I'd ever meet someone who aligns with me, and I also faced anxiety about becoming a mother. If there is anything that I've learned over the past four years, it's that I deserve the absolute best in life, especially in a relationship. It's a bonus, so it should add to my happiness, not subtract from it. I choose not to settle for stuff I don't like.

I found freedom in not falling for a man's words without his actions. If he can't show you what he is telling you, he isn't a man you should believe. Love is an action that is felt more than heard. So if he doesn't treat you right, leave him. No excuses. No lies. No "He just needs time to grow."

No second chances. He's not your plant, and you're not his sun. When we are still finding ourselves, we tend to make a mess out of relationships. Raise your standard of how you treat yourself before looking for love again.

Your Confidence Lies in the Boundaries You Set

When someone is allowed to treat you poorly or damage your self-esteem, you begin to believe all the negative things said about you or that you deserved the treatment received. The way you interact with others is different now. I found myself not trusting people. I questioned everything they said and connected each dot until I perceived I could give them an ounce of my trust. I believed people only wanted to take advantage of me. I believed disappointment was imminent, so isolation was my best friend. Once I was truly okay being alone, this was the next part of my heart that needed healing. Love for me equaled defeat. And in order to not feel that way again, I kept everyone at a distance because I could better manage my feelings. I came off cold or arrogant. When men would walk away, I was okay because I believed they would fail me anyway.

I self-reflect often, so it didn't take me long to recognize my own toxic behavior. Although I can't fully protect myself from getting hurt in the future, I can implement my boundaries or my non-negotiables. Once those lines were crossed, I knew it was time for me to move on.

What are my non-negotiables for dating?

Respect. I do not tolerate disrespect under any circumstances. Because of this, I always give my respect upfront. I will not teach someone how to respect me. This is a character flaw, and you cannot change someone's disposition.

Honesty. I value honesty so much in all of my relationships, not just romantic ones. I am not the person who can't handle the truth. I consider myself to be an honest person, and I am honest with others; anything less is a waste of my time. Give it to me straight, and I'll get a chaser if I need one.

Sincerity. You can't build a solid and genuinely happy relationship if you don't understand the value of sincerity. Being sincere in a relationship means always choosing to feel, act, talk, and react according to your own personal character, your motivations, and your feelings with all honesty and truthfulness.

Infidelity. I understand people make mistakes, and I have made this mistake before. And because I experienced getting an STD in a marriage, I am just tired. I have grown to become a woman with an immense amount of self-control, and I desire that if I am to be serious with someone.

Lack of responsibility or accountability. We are not children. I don't have any children, and I am not trying to raise any adults. This is also a lack of emotional maturity and will often lead to manipulation when conflict arises.

Consistency. This ties in with honesty because if you can't be consistent, then you are not being forthcoming about your feelings and emotions. If a person is not consistent, they are not committed or dedicated to growing a relationship. You will be left feeling confused and frustrated.

Friends with benefits. I am not giving out relationship benefits to someone I am not in a relationship with. I have in the past, and it sounds like a good idea initially. But they always end in drama.

I bring far too much to the fold, and I'm too much of a woman to engage in any type of a "situationship." All of these equate to an unequally yoked dating experience. I'd rather spend my time exploring the depths of my partner and not my time convincing them why they should become a better person. Once you decide people aren't offering you enough, you'll start going after more and expecting it. You will wake up one day and require more in every area of your life. Once you truly believe that you're worthy of it and take action, your life will change, your confidence will change, your willingness to settle for less will change, and what life sends your way will change. The energy alone will cause you to attract better. The key words to creating a boundary are waking up, realizing, wanting more, and taking action.

I receive many messages from various women on social media, most of whom I've never even met. One day, I came across a message where a young lady told me that she is proud of and inspired by my courage...

"I thank you so much for your honesty and transparency in your posts. I am struggling with deciding to end my marriage,

and I feel so embarrassed and silly for everything I've endured in this relationship. He is also a chronic cheater. I am shattered. I want to leave, but it is just so difficult. I don't trust him and I am not sure if I can again. You are so courageous. You give me so much hope that my life, too, will bounce back."

I am still an advocate of marriage. I believe in it. I believe you should fight for it. And I do desire to be married again. But I believe in self-preservation first. Simply stated, some shit just *don't* work out.

What I am not an advocate of is settling. Nobody is going to make me miserable, period. I'm not going to wait fifteen years in hopes it turns around. And ain't no prize for staying in an unhappy marriage just to say, "*We stilllll together.*" That's not my definition of making it. I don't want to begin every single speech about my man saying, "Well, we had our fair share of ups and downs." And I am not talking about life movements—sickness, fertility, death, etc. Life will always do what it does.

Now marriage is work. But it's a different type of work. Staying on one accord is not easy, and you will make many sacrifices, but foolishness and disrespect...I don't want it.

Falling in love with myself and identifying my values were two of the greatest power moves I ever made. It has made boundary setting easier. It made demanding to be treated in alignment with my worth easier. It made refusing to entertain men who I knew were vibrating on frequencies lower than me and would only derail me easier. It made taking care of my mind, body, soul, and spirit easier. It made severing ties with energy vampires easier. It made walking away from shit that no longer served me easier. It made refusing to entertain anything less than reciprocity easier. It made confidence ooze from my pores. It made the scale stand at attention when it calculated my real worth.

Yes, a power move, indeed.

Now this version of me was not born overnight. I was trying to save one fool at a time with the best of them. This is experience. This is pain. This is insecurities. This is guilt. I had to endure and fight to get to this level of confidence today.

Stacey,

You are not negotiating your value with anyone. You're worth it. You've been worth it. You will forever be worth it.

Anastasia

Boundaries give you the courage to understand that you do have power. You actually have more power than you could have imagined.

There are three things you should never feel guilty for:

1. Changing for the better
2. Knowing your worth
3. Staying true to your vision

Even when they can't love you, you are still worthy of love. You've dissected yourself in the mirror too many times for lovers that see you as nothing more than food for their ego. Eventually, I hope you find love that takes the weapons out of your hands and reassures you that you don't have to go to war with yourself for anyone.

The Standards You Set Determines the Life You'll Get

I would rather adjust my life to someone's absence than to adjust my boundaries to accommodate their disrespect. You can walk away from whatever it is that doesn't serve you. The game ends when you stop playing. One thing about me is I don't throw pity parties. This is the reason I've reached the level of mental and emotional maturity that I have today. Growth is never-ending, and once you master where you are currently, there is always a new level waiting to be discovered. Even though I am nowhere near close to where I want to be, I thank God I had the courage to become better and not bitter. Even when I said I was giving up, I kept pushing forward through the growth and healing process no matter how ugly it got.

Stacey,

When we think of "meant to be," we automatically assume forever. But maybe it isn't supposed to last forever. Maybe it's just someone who is in your life to teach you something. Maybe the forever is not the person, but what we gain from them.

Anastasia

Not all relationships or friendships are meant to last. Some are supposed to hurt you to your core, so much so that you commit yourself to never feeling that way again. I've settled for a lot of things because I was uncertain what I wanted. If what you desire is not clear, it is very easy to be distracted by what looks good in the moment. Be intentional and direct in every aspect of your life, not just dating. If you can't decide what it is that you want, you can't begin to think of a plan to get there. If you can't name your values out loud, you can't expect someone else to abide by them.

A few years ago, I decided I wanted to rebuild my life focusing on core values that I believed were the hallmarks of the person I wanted to become. I haven't looked back since.

- Integrity
- Respect
- Humility
- Discipline
- Compassion
- Generosity
- Accountability
- Authenticity

If you can't name the most important values in your life right now, then you certainly can't live by them. You definitely can't expect someone else to. Before you go another day, take some time to ask yourself, "What's most important to me?" "What are the top values in my life?" You need to write them out. If you need to, use Post-it Notes and plaster them in your home or your office. Speak these values to yourself daily and give them life. Until you clarify your values, you can't set your boundaries.

Block Him, Not Your Blessings

Any relationship will require compromise, but not when it comes to your core values. Anything or anyone that jeopardizes the values you have set should not remain in your life. People need to meet you at your level. If they cannot, you will eventually stoop down to theirs. Always remember, a toxic person is more likely to pollute you than you are to purify them, so don't compromise your standards.

> **If you can't name the most important values in your life right now, then you certainly can't live by them.**

I stopped sending paragraphs, stopped begging, and stopped telling people how to treat me. I started walking away, blocking, and distancing myself. Initially, you may think what you feel is loneliness, but it will become peaceful. What you aren't changing, you are choosing. Only you can make the choice to stop entertaining nonsense. When you cut off the baggage, users, and negativity, you begin to surround yourself with people who move like you do. Life is much more satisfying. I don't even give explanations anymore. It's truly not worth it.

Healing doesn't mean the damage never existed. It means the damage no longer controls our lives. I knew I was healing when:

- I started responding rather than reacting.
- I trusted myself and my judgment.
- I enjoyed alone time.
- I saw my parents as people with their own unresolved trauma.
- I set boundaries, and when people didn't respect them, I cleared space for those who did.
- I was okay with being misunderstood.

You cannot heal in the same environment that made you sick. Just because someone doesn't see the value in you that doesn't make you invaluable. People can only do what you allow to be done. Stop wasting time for someone to see you, to match you; you do that for yourself. People will only treat you based on the love and respect you hold toward yourself first. Never let anyone treat you or make you feel like you're small. Take tiny steps every day toward change. Begin your day with reciting your affirmations. One year, I completed a *365 days of self-love* jar. Each day, I wrote down something I loved about myself or something I did that made me proud. After two weeks, I had to think longer and harder. After three months, it was downright difficult. At eight months, I practically gave up, and I only completed the goal because I wanted to be proud of my journey toward valuing myself.

We can blurt out what we don't like about ourselves, yet it takes real effort to think about what we love about ourselves. Make these activities a habit, and don't stop or grow weary. Your consistency in creating a positive environment for yourself will build your confidence to a level you never imagined. If I can elevate the thoughts and opinions I have of myself, so can you. I recognized that the marriage wasn't going to enhance my being. I grew into a woman who had expectations and found a strength to want out. So many women are still surrendering to a life I chose not to live. You can also create a new beginning in any situation. I'd rather live a few years in discomfort than live a life of suffering, knowing I deserved more than the life I settled for.

I hear all the time that women feel not many men know how to appreciate a woman, therefore it is hard to be submissive or give

> **I'd rather live a few years in discomfort than live a life of suffering, knowing I deserved more than the life I settled for.**

him your absolute best version of you. Either the man is unfaithful, makes poor choices, or is not in tune with a woman's emotions. I had this same reasoning in all of my relationships. As a woman of faith, you are only to be submissive to a husband who is God-fearing. If you are married to a man that is not God-fearing, I would suggest marital and family counseling to begin the process of moving in the direction toward Christ.

If a man doesn't know how to appreciate you, why would you be with him? Why stay with a man who is cheating on you? Why stay with a man who cannot be honest? You show how much you value yourself by not being in any relationship where you are not appreciated. Someone who isn't concerned about you and your feelings shouldn't have access to you. This is a lack of boundaries. I believe many women have a hard time being submissive because our first thought is, "Why would I be submissive to a man that doesn't treat me right or makes bad decisions?" The real question should be, "Why would I be in a relationship with a man who does these things in the first place?"

Stacey,

I forgive you for ignoring your worth in hopes of changing someone else's mind about you.

Anastasia

We often say in reference to men, "Stop disturbing women you are not ready for." Better yet, "Stop allowing yourself to be disturbed." Stop allowing your time to be wasted. We KNOW when he ain't on nothing—we're just hoping he changes! We must become accountable for the ways we allow others to treat us. We hope that if we show him how great of a woman we are, he will magically get his act together in order to not lose us. You may not have lost the relationship, but you have already lost the battle. We should not change for someone else; we should change for ourselves and ourselves only. That is sustainable change. Someone changing for you is shifty, and you should not want nor ask for that. We give other individuals way too much credit over our lives and our happiness. We are more in control than we think. We possess more power than we give ourselves credit for. As women, we have the power to create life, so we have more than enough power to create the life we want. My heart hurts for the girl I was six years ago. The girl who was begging for someone to treat her better than she treated herself. The girl who constantly was proving her worth. The girl who questioned why she wasn't good enough. And the girl who didn't have the power to leave at the first sign of trouble. Never again will I question my own self-worth over someone else, but God redeems all time. Not only did He restore me, He evolved me.

If you don't currently possess the qualities you seek, how are you expecting to receive it in return? Not everyone needs to have access to you while you're healing, restoring, growing, and transforming. Protecting certain phases of your process will be required in order to elevate and self-actualize—successfully. This means stop dating when you are vibrating at a low frequency. It affects your ability to choose quality partners. You could potentially find yourself with someone who is compatible with your dysfunction. You stand the risk of rushing your healing process due to loneliness and not give yourself the attention you need to transform. Be so committed to what's best for your heart that you're willing to sit through the most uncomfortable pain of growth and change. Refuse to accept anything less than complete love and alignment.

Stacey,

You've made magic out of your wounds, and that gives you every right to be cautious about who is allowed to experience you. The fruits of your healing are not for everyone to bite into.

Anastasia

Once women realize men don't determine their value or worth, that God does, they glow differently. There is something so serious and so crucial about a light that can't be dimmed by another person. Sometimes we go through things that cause us to lose our spark, but baby, when you get back up, make sure you rise as the whole goddamn fire.

FOOLISH FAITH

God isn't going to give you someone who doesn't support the vision He gave you for your life. They'll fit the vision. Anything else is a distraction. And not only will they fit it, they will magnify it. You know how it feels to get with someone that doesn't flow with your rhythm; everything is out of whack! This person will be a true addition to your healing.

It takes people coming and going. It takes painful moments. It takes discovery and vulnerability. It takes digging in and learning oneself. It takes hurt to reveal our greatest opportunities to grow and experience freedom within. We can't have growth without being present to what life throws our way. And we can't have growth if there aren't experiences that demand us to look closely at ourselves and our relationships. Embrace what comes and what leaves you. Embrace the pain and remind yourself that it's calling you to something...if you let it. You don't just arrive. You won't just arrive. You must work for it. This glory doesn't come easy.

Boundaries are not selfish, they are an act of self-love. One day, you will believe that the love you give is also the love you deserve. May you be brave enough to choose yourself, even when others don't.

Have you congratulated yourself for the progress no one knows about? Take that bow.

TRUTH JOURNAL

TRUTH JOURNAL

_____
_____
_____
_____
_____
_____
_____
_____
_____
_____
_____
_____
_____
_____
_____
_____
_____

CHAPTER EIGHT

DECIDING WHO YOU ARE MEANS DECIDING WHO YOU WILL NEVER BE AGAIN

> *"Don't copy the behavior and customs of this world, but let God transform you into a new person by changing the way you think."*
>
> — Romans 12:2 New Living Translation

SELF-LOVE MEANS TELLING yourself, gently and firmly, "You are in my way; kindly step aside."

The relationship you have with yourself is the most complicated because you can't walk away from you. Wherever your journey may lead you, you must take YOU (mindset) with you. You have to forgive every mistake. You have to deal with every flaw. Even in a season when you are disgusted with yourself, you must find a way to love you.

One of the hardest skills to master is saying no to yourself so that you can rise up and unfold into a greater version. Saying no to yourself looks like this:

- Saying no to distractions or lack of consistency
- Saying no to the patterns or ways of being that only lead back to the past
- Saying no to only doing what is easy
- Saying no to love that is beneath you
- Saying no to doubt and fear

This battle is not against who we have been. It is an all-out war against who we are becoming.

You did the BEST you could do with what you had at the time. You did your best with all the knowledge, the emotions, the finances, the skills, even the love you had. Forgive yourself for where you THINK you fell short because, in reality, you didn't. Find peace that you are better equipped now.

You can't detox an entire decade in a day, or a year for that matter. Be patient with yourself. The greatest things take time to build. Much of our effort comes from putting our own foot down and saying enough is enough.

Growth isn't always constant. Relapses happen. You're not back at square one. Your growth prior to your relapse isn't erased. Take your time. Don't be so hard on yourself. You will relapse on your self-discovery journey. It is absolutely okay! You will learn every time you regress to your old habits, reactions, thoughts, and emotions, and you will be reminded of the very place you don't want to go back to. You'll learn because YOU, my dear, you're determined to be the best version of yourself! Every day you've been stepping past your comfort zone. The woman you are today got you through all you've ever been through.

The day you finally let go of the person you've been pointlessly holding on to is the day your life gets a whole lot better. Appreciate yourself. Forgive yourself. And also learn to forgive family, friends, and past lovers. My parents were unable to teach me what they didn't know. I was hurt until I realized that I knew better, therefore, I could do better and make better choices for the next generation. My friends hurt me because we weren't able to handle the rollercoaster of emotions during disagreements. And my exes hurt me by not valuing me or what I brought to the relationship. No one may have intended to hurt me. We are all doing the best we can with what we have. However, when a man does wrong by a woman, it doesn't always mean he doesn't know her worth. It means he also doesn't know his own. In all of these instances, we are simply collateral damage in someone else's war against themselves. So stop looking for closure because the only thing it can give you is an excuse. If they're not convicted within themselves, how can they have remorse toward you? Forgive without the apology and move on with your life. Is it unfair? Yes, but this isn't a Broadway play. This ain't a dress rehearsal; this is your real life. Every single day, you must show up for yourself even when others don't. You don't need closure; you need to HEAL! I had to learn that forgiveness is for myself and an apology from someone else should not determine doing the work necessary to mend my own heart.

Stacey,

You can decide at any time you want a different kind of life. Make a list of all the things you want. Figure out who you truly want to become. Ask yourself what needs to be done to make it happen. Then put yourself in that place. No more excuses. You are up to you.

Anastasia

The more I pay attention, the more life's circumstances present opportunity for growth and depth. I ask questions, and when my ego or fear answers, I recognize it. I cry. I write. I reflect. I learn. Gratitude awakes. Then the cycle begins all over again. Getting to know yourself feels scarier than all else because on the other side you are left with YOU, whoever that is, in all of its forms. In the process of getting to know myself again, I felt a sense of fear because I constantly placed my happiness in the hands of other people. This was my comfortable place. To no longer be able to place blame on an individual meant that a life of mediocrity would solely reflect on my ability to persevere, or not.

We all know someone who still blames their shortcomings or broken heart on someone who hurt them or left them years ago. No one else is responsible for your own happiness or success in life but you. Not discovering yourself is far more of a fearful burden that ultimately stops you from living your life to its fullest. Self-love is true freedom. I'd rather not miss out on that, and I don't think you should either. This constant seesaw that happens within each of us is the thread that connects all of us—that truth must remind us to be kind to our fellow sisters and to lead with love with ourselves.

If You Won't Let the Past Die, Then It Won't Let You Live

You can't get ready for your future by staring at your past. Your gaze is holding you back. You keep looking backwards and wonder why you're still stumbling. You can't get over what happened, what you've been through, and how unjust it was. And you're right. It was very unjust, but I promise you that looking backwards will never get you to better yourself. Stop projecting things on to yourself that are false narratives. What is true is that you didn't know who you were. You didn't know what you carried. You denied your own mistakes. You didn't know that you are a force of a woman, and you got led astray.

Living in my past kept me comfortable, stagnant, and it eliminated any sense of accountability to take control of my own life. I focused on what I didn't receive in my childhood until I realized I was the agent of change for my own children. I was frustrated in the lack of growth I experienced in the early years of my career until I discovered my own gifts and passions. I stayed stuck because what I had wasn't what I wanted even though it was enough for what I needed in the moment. It's easy to stay in a relationship where you are miserable so you can blame that man for wasting your best years. I learned through my marriage that things will become exactly as you see them. My trust was violated. In order to create some false sense of control, I kept others at arm's length in order to not be wounded again. No, they weren't honest. People that struggle to be honest with us are struggling to be honest with themselves. We are just an extension of their inner experience. We will continue to encounter people who are dishonest; it happens. However, if you cage yourself, you will never be free.

Stacey,

You cannot hope to heal when you are stuck between needing to get over them and still wishing they would come back. Don't reopen your heart for toxic people, and call it seeking closure. Forgiveness does not require reconnection.

Anastasia

One of the hardest things I've had to understand is that closure comes from within. Especially difficult if you've been betrayed by someone you love because you feel like you must let them know the pain they've caused. For months I wondered if my ex would ever reach out to me and apologize. I was infuriated that he had the nerve not to recognize or admit the hurt and damage he caused me. I would get upset when I saw him living his "best life" while I was trying to figure out my next moves. Then one day I had an epiphany, that he wasn't living in this space anymore, so why am I? Why am I allowing this situation to take over my heart so that I cannot move on with my life? An apology changes absolutely nothing. It likely wouldn't have even made me feel better. So I finally decided to quit re-reading the pages of that chapter. The temptation to become bitter, hard, and do people like they've done you is soooo juicy. I get it. For once, you'd like to treat others how they have treated you or someone else would do the dirty work. You may have gotten some hot tea to gossip about, but I promise it won't heal your broken heart. What will heal is forgiveness of yourself and the other person and doing the work. The peace you seek can only be given to you by you. HEAL...so you can experience the life God desires for you without the filter of your wound. I didn't realize how much I was carrying until I put it all down. What consumes your mind ultimately controls your life. I preach values, respect, and accountability so much because life doesn't coddle you. If you fall down, you must pick yourself back up. It doesn't matter how you got there, and, regardless of fault, nobody will save you. You must get up and change your mind. If you don't, that is nobody's fault but your own. As I began to forgive myself, it became easier to forgive others.

Getting your life together requires a level of honesty you can't even imagine. There is nothing easy about realizing you're the one that's been holding you back this entire time. Life will give you whatever experience YOU need for the evolution of your consciousness and your growth. Hence the word YOU. That is why you cannot pay attention to someone else's tests and trials and wonder "Why me?" and "Why not them?" What they're experiencing, YOU may not need. Our trials are to make us better individually. To give us strength in areas we are weak. To help us overcome challenges we didn't know we needed. How do you know this is the experience you need? Because God allowed this experience to happen to you in this moment to change you at your core.

To question God about your place in life is to question His sovereignty. Of course, I wish that God had told me that it would take this long before I saw the movement I was looking for. Maybe I would have utilized the time better. Maybe not. What is there to gain if we always get what we ask for? Character is built in unanswered prayers. The truth of who you are is revealed in unanswered prayers. Who are you when you don't get your way? The struggle teaches you what you don't want to return to and helps you appreciate all that you do have. We experience problems so God can get our attention and show us that we're headed in the wrong direction.

Our life's lessons will last as long as they need to until we get it. Sometimes the journey is longer for our protection. There are things we've been kept from and spared from because God took the scenic route. Shortcuts aren't always our friend. He still has to prepare us for all that we've prayed for. We all want to be the first to do or achieve something. It helps us to feel better about ourselves and the present situation. Acquiring something fast or reaching a "destination" first isn't always what's best for us. God knows this. He slows our travels because if we get it too fast, we will forget we ever needed God in the first place. Whether it takes one year, two, or ten, His timing is perfect. You will always arrive on time to what He has for you. Please don't be in a rush to receive less than God's best. You will only wish you had waited and trusted His guidance.

Good Enough Is Not What's Best for You. Never Settle.

You become what you surround yourself with. Energy is transferable and contagious. Your environment will consume you. When women like us rise above certain incidents and decide to heal ourselves, our insistence on joy is a threat to those who devalued us. Had I stayed married, I wouldn't be happy. I wouldn't be writing. I wouldn't have rediscovered lost hobbies. I wouldn't have confidence. I wouldn't have discovered my true essence. I wouldn't have taken back control over my life. It took a failed marriage and a season in the valley to project me right into my purpose. When I played small, I didn't have to face my own insecurities. There is a pressure that comes with being center stage, not from a popularity point of view, but from a breakthrough point of view. When you have a breakthrough, you simply cannot go back to being small or ordinary. It is very possible to experience a breakdown and a breakthrough simultaneously. Some people prefer to experience you in the way that keeps them most comfortable. When you're not growing, they're not forced to either. It's a hard realization to swallow. Sometimes God will minimize your circle in order for you to draw close to Him. I think the most difficult thing about this phase for me was being misunderstood. Occasionally, you can feel like you're on an island by yourself. I cannot base who I am on how others act around me. Consistency in who I am is what will move the mountain. Meet people where they are but show up as you every single time.

Stacey,

Some won't understand the work you did emotionally to get HERE, and that's okay.

Anastasia

FOOLISH FAITH

Your growth doesn't owe anyone an explanation or an apology. Different stages of your life will come with different familiarity and different understanding. People will stop understanding you at certain phases in your advancement. Growth comes in many forms, and sometimes it's difficult to recognize in the face of another individual. They no longer see themselves within you. If you've outgrown their comfort level, you shouldn't take it personally. You are a version they have yet to meet in themselves. Even in your discomfort, God will always send your tribe when you need it.

A major problem I've noticed women face during a person of isolation is denying the fact that they're hurt. We often try to portray that we don't care or that we are not affected by our experiences or the changes that are taking place in our lives. This is the problem: by 'acting' like you don't care, you are prolonging your healing process. It is important to be honest about how you feel and honest about your transformation. If you are hurt, admit it. If you want to cry, cry. This is what makes us human and is our essence as women to nurture and care. Although we cannot live in this mental state for very long, there is no need to be ashamed of being in pain. Accepting that you are hurting will allow the emotions to play out naturally, and therefore your healing process will not be forced. When it is forced, the pain will come back and hit you when you least expect it. Even in pain, you are still beautiful and powerful.

There is no purpose of experiencing that much pain, misery, and anxiety to receive no profit. To have been shattered and get no gain or anything out of it makes your years of that experience in vain and invaluable. Do not sabotage yourself. In order to grow from a painful experience, focus your mind on your recovery. Forget the mistake, and elevate in your lesson. If you take nothing else, make sure that whatever situation you walk away from makes you stronger, wiser, better, and WHOLE.

Accountability is empowering. When you're not ready to acknowledge your own behavior, it feels like an attack. Accountability stops you from playing the victim and puts you in a position to win. Are you willing to leave behind the way you talk? Are you willing to leave behind the way you think about your story? Many will not, and that's why they never have a new experience. Self-sabotage is knowing what you need to do to improve and not doing it. We make excuses, which are just our own limiting beliefs in disguise. Many times we sabotage ourselves to remain small and safe. Are you ready to do the scary things that will improve your life? Are you ready to make decisions based on your actual worth? We can either choose prosperity and advancement or we can choose to be stagnant and mediocre. But we can't live in these places at the same time.

It is important to spend time unraveling what isn't working for us and *within* us to make room for what does. In order to get to where we are going, we must continually challenge ourselves to release mediocre versions of ourselves. Below are a few examples of ways we self-sabotage from achieving our innermost desires.

- Show up as a false, edited, watered-down, pleasing, accommodating, selfless, managed version of yourself *and* want to feel accepted, embraced, and seen for who you truly are at your core
- Give away all your energy to external sources *and* expect to find energy for yourself
- Numb, suppress, and hide what's true *and* find liberation from being honest
- Ask God for signs of direction *and* ignore those same signs when they appear
- Put your worth outside of yourself *and* fully live into your innate worthiness
- Try to be for everyone *and* be fully, wholly yourself
- Cling to control where you don't have it *and* accept what is
- Be over-committed to your pain *and* make plenty of room for your joy
- Believe you will never change *and* give yourself the opportunity to change
- Follow other people's ideas of what the best or most true choice for your is *and* follow your own blueprint in life

When you begin to discover yourself, your desires become very specific. Having and/or accepting just anything won't do. Don't ignore your spirit when it is trying to guide you away from situations that are unhealthy for you. Below are a few really hard questions I asked of myself that really opened my heart to see how I was *still* sabotaging myself, even in the midst of my healing. I wanted to ensure that once I rediscovered who I am, I would become unstoppable.

Are there things I am expecting to happen in my life that aren't possible in the way I am allowing myself to exist? I expected my uncommunicated expectations to miraculously be met. No one can read our minds, and we must stop expecting them to. Instead of being upset with myself for my lack of communication as the reason I never received what I needed from others, I would become irritable with those who couldn't hear my plea from my closed lips. Uncommunicated expectations never get met. Speak what you seek, so that you may see what you said. You can't be offended by not getting something you never had the courage to ask for.

Am I living in a way that subtly confirms to myself that I'm not deserving of what's possible? I have allowed myself to wallow in guilt. I realized that other people were not my problem, but indeed I was. The choices I have made in life led me to begin self-loathing. I would make faint statements like, "Oh, my moment has passed, I should have done that by now," or "If I only didn't make that mistake, I wouldn't be in this place." I would listen to inspiring messages to lift my mood, but in actuality I did not think God was going to redeem or restore me. I began to believe that I couldn't persevere. I disqualified myself. My thoughts never aligned with my actions. I spoke positively with friends and colleagues, but I didn't believe a word I said. I worked extremely hard, but never saw any movement or momentum. Life or death lies in the power of our tongue. It wasn't until I was sick of feeling this way that I asked God for forgiveness. If you go back to fix all the mistakes you ever made, you will erase yourself. Nothing you've done is so bad that God isn't right there to breathe His breath of life into you. Our past versions are what makes everything we have possible today.

Where am I trying to do two things at once that might be cancelling each other out? I have spent years expecting to be understood and heard without showing up as my fullest self which, of course, prevented me from being heard or misunderstood. I did this out of fear of conflict, and fear that people would perceive me as being "too much." Ironically, I was still very much misunderstood, and I even found myself secretly upset at those who misunderstood a false version of myself. Crazy, right?

Is there anything I might shift, pivot, or change today that would feel deeper in alignment with who I actually am? I needed to learn to stop having sympathy for people who are uncomfortable or have a dislike for me or my presence. I started speaking boldly about my wants and desires in all relationships, not just romantic ones. I stopped holding back out of fear of someone not rising to meet me on my level. Everyone will not be for you, nor remain in your life longer than a season. I allowed myself to mourn the loss of those people as long as I needed to in order to heal.

You Are the Greatest Project You Will Ever Work On. Create Magic

I have always believed that the people we attract are a reflection of the energy we put out. What we accept is a reflection of how we feel about ourselves. What we think we deserve and what we deal with comes down to our decision-making. People see how they should treat you based on the values you hold yourself to. We MUST (yes, it is that serious) make sure our actions align with our intentions. The reason you have a hard time trusting your intuition is because you are still convinced that some outside authority knows better than you. When I started taking myself seriously, people acted accordingly. When I decided I was done wasting my time, people started dropping like flies. When you set a new standard, you will realize how many of those benefitted from your lack of self-love and boundaries.

You can't be out here saying you want something real, but you are settling for whoever comes your way and acts right just long enough to get you hooked. I know how hard this is because no one wants to be alone, but seeking validation from someone else is not the answer. The love you have for someone else should never come at the expense of the love that you have for yourself. You have to get really good at being good to you. Make choices that serve you. Listen to your spirit and act on what it whispers. Release yourself from relationships that require you to perform a role. Our own changed behavior is the answer to many of our prayers.

My divorce produced a resilience inside of me. I should have lost my mind. I should have been angry. I should have been bitter. I should have been depressed. When you are willing to get uncomfortable and expand your customary ways of thinking, you fundamentally change your life. Watching Him move in ways that are different from what you hope or envision, you will see He was making you into the grandest version of you to handle all of the blessings He has in store. The journey took longer than I anticipated, but it is what was best because it ultimately changed me. We want the glory without going through the process and without being made uncomfortable. We love to indulge in our insecurities. It feels humble. But what it does is give us an excuse not to fulfill our calling or to be present in our now, in our reality. We like comfortability. So rather than rise to the level God desires for us, we retreat to our insecurities. When I ultimately submitted myself to God's way, I experienced God's will.

Stacey,

This heartbreak saved your life. You and your ex not working out was favor. You don't see it yet, but one day you will. Your brokenness is your blessing. I'm excited to see the person you're becoming. I am already proud of you.

Anastasia

Healing was never meant to be easy. It requires us to be wounded first. If there isn't a wound, there's nothing to heal from. And if there isn't healing, you can't grow. To meet new parts of ourselves means we must lose old parts first. Wounds and trauma are no fun, but the reality is you can't heal without them. You can't deepen your relationship with yourself without your trials. A faith that hasn't been tested can't be trusted. If you walk an unwounded life, there's no story to tell. It is what connects us to the people in this world who need our story, our resiliency, our vulnerability, and our growth. It's not meant to be easy. It's meant to be courageous and brave. It's meant to be demanding. It's meant to need your attention and be hard work. The wounds are always bringing you closer to yourself, never further away.

This new life you want to manifest will require more than you ever thought possible. The version of myself that is writing this book had to give up the version that was married. Even the version that was newly divorced. It cost me my comfort zone and sense of direction. It cost me a marriage, relationships, and friendships. It cost me being liked and misunderstood. It even cost me my sense of self as everything I grew to believe about me was still not what God said about me.

You don't just wake up and become a butterfly. You first must "un-become." Un-becoming is even more important than becoming. Whatever you're praying to walk into, you must be able to walk out of where you are to get there. You have to be honest and say, "God, I want to walk into your promises, but I am struggling to walk out of what I've been familiar with for so long." Comfort and destiny will not coexist. You will need to make up your mind, so I suggest you do it at this moment. Are you going to be everything God said you could be? Or will you find comfort in discomfort?

Broken Girls Become Unstoppable Women

My most powerful moment was when I decided I wasn't the person who was in the situation. I wasn't the person looking back at me in the mirror. I don't ever want to be her again.

I didn't want to be that old Stacey anymore. The old Stacey was insecure. The old Stacey had anxiety. The old Stacey didn't trust herself. The old Stacey settled. I remember when I started praying to God to stretch me and reveal His will for my life. My world, as I knew it, immediately began to fall apart, and I couldn't understand it. When you ask God to go to the next level, don't be surprised when every person or situation preventing your progress is removed.

Sometimes, the answers to your prayers are what you lose. Many people believe the answers to their prayers are the result of them gaining something. No, sometimes it is about loss and losing the shit that holds you down. Sometimes you've got to lose that job to get the dream career or start the business you've been begging God for. Sometimes you have to lose your significant other in order to receive your soul mate. Sometimes you have to lose your entire mind in order to gain clarity and peace.

God will disappoint you on one level so you can dream bigger, think bigger, and be bigger on the next level. Stop being afraid to lose things and start over. It just shows that you aren't ready to receive what you are asking for.

The first step in recognizing who you are is knowing who you are not. That amazing transition and transformation that you're looking for will come from you making a solid decision and taking action. I am often asked, "How do I change something I know is unhealthy?" And my response is always, "By understanding why you are choosing it in the first place." I've discovered that we want to know how to do better. We are eager to learn how to make things right, make better choices, set boundaries, and live authentically. We want to choose the best partner and friends. We want the most fulfilling career. We want to learn how to deal with our unhealthy family dynamics. But we can't really learn the new without understanding the old. We have to understand where we are first.

FOOLISH FAITH

We have to see ourselves in the old patterns as part of the equation. We have to see the wounds that subconsciously guide us. We have to acknowledge our old patterns and firewalls that we've developed to deal with dysfunctional dynamics. Understanding who you are right now is the only way to a new you. Start examining and uncovering the layers that are currently guiding you. This is how you build the foundation for growth.

Even in your lowest moments, growth is still a possibility. Even in the midst of ashes, life will begin again. So if you feel like it's over, it's really just a new beginning. You never know how life's devastations can be used to "grow" you in new ways. The reality is, I didn't truly love my ex even though I loved him hard. I loved who I painted him to be. I loved the idea of "us" and what he could become. If I had accepted him for who he really was, I wouldn't have loved him at all.

I hope that you are becoming more comfortable with yourself. Not just the self you know. Not the self you may have, for some reason or another, settled for. When I say be yourself, I mean the self that whispers brilliant ideas to you before bed. The self that loves courageously, the self that takes risks, and the self that believes in fairy tales, magical thinking, and powerful planning. The self you know and the self that exists on the other side of your fear and beyond your wildest dreams.

This level of womanhood will require you to rise to the occasion at all times instead of in waves. This level means choosing happiness over history and never looking back. Stop pretending you are oblivious to make other people comfortable in their ignorance. I'm not going to abandon what I know so you can feel better about yourself. When you refuse to know better, everyone suffers.

May we all have the courage to say no to what does not serve our highest good. Say "yes" to what lifts us up into greater freedom, "yes" to harmony in relationships, and "yes" to bringing ourselves into the present moment so we can experience personal joy.

I pray that God comes through in the very area you thought was impossible. I pray that your silent prayers are answered with no more delays. I pray that you will withstand the process of transformation. I pray that your mourning turns into heavy shouts of praise. I pray that your hope is restored with the desires of your heart...even the ones you may have forgotten.

Beautiful woman, can't you see that you need you?

TRUTH JOURNAL

TRUTH JOURNAL

CHAPTER NINE

QUEENS ARE NOT BORN; THEY ARE AWAKENED

> *"For God does not give us a spirit of fear and timidity, but of power, love, and self-discipline."*
>
> — 2 Timothy 1:7 New Living Translation

IMAGINE THE MOST brave, confident, at peace, happiest version of you. Now start showing up as her…today.

This new version of yourself doesn't have to wait until your birthday, next year, or even next week. If you are still in love with your comfort zone, those dates mean nothing. Year after year, you will continue to fight the same battles. You can begin where you are right now. It doesn't matter how old you are or what you should have done five years ago. Don't let a timeline become the catalyst for your growth. YOU are the spark that you always needed.

Since we all love memes (girl, I love a good meme), there is one that I know holds true: "I didn't get anything I prayed for until I became the type of person who should receive it." We are fully capable of receiving everything we desire, but it begins with us first. We must first change our own minds and habits.

RIP to All the Times I Almost Quit

God will disrupt your entire life just to speak to you. I was okay with losing all that I had so that I could gain again. You never know who you are until you are attacked. When your back is against the wall and everything is riding on you, that is when you see yourself push through like never before. That's why God allowed you in the fight—to discover yourself.

When it comes to following our dreams, sometimes the hardest thing to do is just START. We come up with so many reasons as to why we haven't or can't start yet. We are not ready, waiting for the right moment, our product is not perfect yet, we don't know enough, don't have enough money, don't have enough resources, don't have enough time...the list goes on! I want you to just start. Just do it! Start before you think you are ready. Start in imperfection. Start with what you have and where you are. You can either be afraid to do it, or you can do it afraid. Be passionate and learn as you go. When I got started in real estate, I completely switched industries. I knew NOTHING. I was so extremely nervous about marketing myself; I was a secret agent for almost two years. I only closed deals with people I knew, which gave me the slight confidence I needed to keep at it. I was in a full-time career that depressed me and, quite frankly, I simply didn't know how long I was going to make it there! Knowing this, I studied everything about the real estate purchase and sale contract. I can recite it verbatim. I came up with a social media marketing plan. To get comfortable connecting with strangers, I started hosting open houses. I made sure I was so knowledgeable about the process that they could trust me with their biggest asset. Do what you have to do to make it work. The key is you must start somewhere!

Don't dig up in doubt what you've planted in faith. Self-doubt is your biggest enemy! In order to get over myself, I had to push through my own perception. Other people do not often see the flaws we think exist, and we hold ourselves back for years believing a false narrative! I started making sure that I always had my business cards with me whenever I went out so I could make new connections. There are tons of realtors out there, many of whom were closing deals left and right and had a bigger sphere and platform than I did as I was just getting started. I could have stayed intimidated, but I wasn't going to allow that to stop me from putting myself out there. I wasn't an influencer, and I had no real business experience, but I was knowledgeable. I knew my contracts front to back, and I believed in myself. I don't care how many people do what I do. I don't care how many homes or how many books they sell. They don't do it like me. They don't do it with my brain, my ethics, my style, my authenticity, my values, or my heart. Your passion is all you need.

What's Easy Won't Change You

It is difficult to become confident in yourself. Social media makes it look easy and sometimes even glamorous, but it's not. My struggle toward self-confidence and self-love is constantly evolving. In my experience, self-loathing doesn't miraculously go away. It takes work. Showing up for that work is what's most important. Some days are better than others, but the battle begins every morning you wake up. You will fail some days. There were days I couldn't find the motivation no matter how hard I looked for it. You have to go back to the drawing board daily, read your affirmations *out loud,* and release the emotions of mishaps and failures from yesterday. As you manage the turbulence of evolution, self-love and compassion is extremely necessary to get you to what you long for...peace.

Define what happiness means and looks like to you, and not anyone else. When we typically answer this question, we answer it materialistically. When I was in the very beginning of operating my business, I thought that if I could just make one or two sales along with my 9-5 income I would be satisfied. Or once I finally could re-furnish my apartment, I would be happy. Once I got those things, I increased my sales goal and then I wanted a condo! And all of that is perfectly fine; we should always want to grow, increase, and achieve the lifestyles we desire. But on the way to achieving our goals, we should still experience joy in our everyday lives. I would get stressed and frustrated every time I was in-between a new level. We think that we can't and won't be happy until we receive something on the other side, but we must make the decision to be happy in who we are, where we are, and in the season we are in. Motivation such as awards, praise, money, etc., have a relatively short lifespan and tend to lead to an endless cycle of needing more in order to stay happy. You do need a combination of both external and internal motivation; however, extrinsic motivation shouldn't be your only source.

When it relates to happiness, here is an example of our mindsets:

Destructive Mindset:

"Once I achieve X, then I will be happy with myself and my life."

Constructive Mindset:

"I feel good about myself and my life now, and achieving X will only add to it."

How often do we correlate our happiness to something, and once we FINALLY receive it, we are already looking for the next thing? And while waiting for that next thing to happen, we become unhappy again? I just KNEW that once I got a new job, I would be so happy because I could finally pay off a few things and be able to engage in more social activities. But once I elevated my lifestyle, that new position wasn't working for me anymore. I paid off my credit card debt, but I also moved into a nicer apartment, so I needed more money. My paycheck was stretched like it was previously. Wanting to upgrade my life and my career wasn't the issue. But once those upgrades became my normal, I fell back into the unhappiness pattern. It's counterproductive. We always get what we want in due time. In actuality, you get exactly what you ask for then you realize you have to get better at asking.

Stacey,

When you focus on what works for you instead of what doesn't, you step out of that comparison cycle and spiral into your real, beautiful life.

Anastasia

It is so easy to live our lives saying, "I'm just waiting on God to move." Reality is, He's waiting on you. All along, He's been waiting on you to prepare for what you are praying for. God truly does us a favor in making us wait. If God gave us what we were praying for at the time we wanted it, we would have messed it all up. We couldn't handle both the greatness and the burden of the blessing at the time we said the prayer. God is waiting on your character to catch up with what you are believing and praying for. God has a major purpose for your life, but are you ready? Is your integrity on point? If God opened the door to that major platform, could you stay humble when the crowds are seeking you out? Or would it go to your head? Once we start receiving our blessings, we can't forget that we need God as much if not more. Can you handle people you know personally or those you don't know at all speaking negatively about you? Or is your clapback button so strong that people would miss what God is doing through you? Can you handle the responsibility? If God brought you that spouse you've been praying for right now, are you ready to forgive and love even when your flesh wants to fight?

> **God has a major purpose for your life, but are you ready?**

Are You Sure YOU Are Not the Weapon Formed Against You?

It's not the enemy. It's YOU. Your only limitations are those you impose on yourself. How long will you allow self-doubt to hold you captive? You are worthy of all that you dream and hope for. One of the most life-awakening things you can do is recognize you are your own poison. Your mindset is the hater you should be referring to, not that girl on Facebook. You are your biggest hater. YOU take being your own worst critic to another level. Stop being negative about everything that has the potential to be positive. Self-pity is easily the most destructive, non-pharmaceutical narcotic. It's addictive, it gives momentary pleasure, and it separates the victim from reality.

Many of us can't reach a successful peak because we are programmed to look at the glass half empty rather than half full. You see how far away you are from the goal rather than seeing all of your accomplishments toward attaining that goal. I always saw how much further I had to go, and how far behind I thought I was from everyone else. When we compare ourselves to others, we never truly consider the fullness of all they may have gone through or experienced, we only consider the parts of them that we deem as good or better, with little to no knowledge of the other parts to them that make them a whole imperfect being. Comparison is not only the thief of joy within ourselves, it is the disrupter of joy within our relationships. Overcoming comparison begins with learning to love the parts of ourselves that we've pushed away, dislike or have deemed unworthy while learning to honor the fullness of others.

FOOLISH FAITH

If you gather enough faith in the Lord, He will grant you the mental clarity to realize that what you perceive as a setback is actually a blessing in disguise. If you don't develop the mental stamina to hold on when the going gets treacherous, you will give up and miss the wisdom and strength God has intended for you on your journey. It took years for me to acknowledge the things I was actually able to achieve in a time where I thought I was suffering. Or who I became through my suffering, which is most important.When you refuse to learn, when you don't believe, when you are cynical, there will be gaps in your life. These gaps will hold you back from leaping ahead in any facet of your journey. To avoid this, *BELIEVE*—even when it feels almost impossible.

When you become impatient, it reveals your doubt in God's perfect timing. God certainly has a plan for your life, and sometimes waiting on Him can feel like watching paint dry, but He is never in a hurry. It's so easy to forget because we want results almost instantly, so we take matters into our own hands. When you dwell in guilty feelings, it reveals your unbelief in God's forgiveness. This is the primary reason we can't forgive ourselves, and our guilt holds us captive. When you become resentful or bitter, it reveals that you doubt God's wisdom. Things won't always turn out how we plan or want, but we can't convince ourselves our situation will always be this way. And you don't believe He can make good out of bad.

When it pertains to relationships, women sometimes say, "All men are dogs." Typically, this means they have given up. It typically means that instead of searching their own hearts and considering that they've picked poorly one too many times, they'd rather place the blame elsewhere. Great men exist, but it's time we take some accountability. We can't ignore the signs and then allow a "no-good" type to come into our lives and cause chaos. I am in no way letting men off the hook. We can't consistently pick wrong, allow too much access to our bodies and our hearts too soon just to scream, "All men are dogs!" Yes, some are dogs, but tell me you didn't hear them barking? He may not have been able to love you, but if we're being honest you didn't love yourself. Let's save ourselves first and fall in love again; this time we'll do it right.

Authenticity Is the Ultimate Currency

An authentic path may take longer, but the moves and impact are forever legendary. If you are unhappy, it is because you are not being authentic. You are not in alignment with who you are. This is not because of anyone else. To be authentic, you have to be you, and you have to go all in on that. You will not become great at what you do until you are great at who you are. You are a gift. Your presence is a gift. When you attempt to be someone else, it not only means you're an imposter, but it also means that you are too afraid to be yourself. Don't live in that fear anymore. Your authentic self is totally acceptable and welcome. That's the only version of you the world can benefit from. You can only sell you, so sell yourself! We get no value out of a counterfeit version of someone who already exists.

> **You will not become great at what you do until you are great at who you are.**

I am an introvert, but I live in an extrovert world. Whenever I feel pressure to "turn up" to match the energy of a room, I remind myself to never let the room I'm in define who I am. I recognize that I have the power of making the room adjust to my truth. You can level up in your truth. You can experience major growth without folding on your principles and values! Don't be held hostage to someone else's expectation or definition of you from individuals who cannot relate to your circumstances.

Stacey,

The reason you just can't settle is because you know what God spoke to you. You're scared, but you're being ushered into a season where you simply can't fake it anymore. You're beginning to really understand who you are. That's your worth breaking through. You're royalty.

Anastasia

Once I got over my own embarrassment, I realized there are other women out there like me who needed to hear what I had to say. I am not a woman of many words, so I never put a lot of confidence into my own voice. I was always the girl in class who was afraid to speak up, even if I knew the answer. I was comfortable being in the back and keeping my opinion to myself because I didn't find my own thoughts to be considered valuable. I sabotaged myself and my growth for a very long time. There is no wrong way to be yourself. You cannot simply say the wrong things, act the wrong way, or make the wrong choices when you are being authentic to your true self. Stop playing small. Stop pretending you don't own the place. Stop dimming your light because you think it's more polite. Shed your insecurity and own it.

Being yourself inspires others to do the same. I am often asked, "How do you start sharing your story?" as if there is a magic potion or perfect time. There isn't. It's incredible how many things we've gone through that can help other people, but we never speak about it because we are too ashamed. I kept myself hostage because of shame. People can write a book in a month—a couple of weeks even. There is no reason this should have taken me three years; I was simply too embarrassed. I pretended like I wasn't called to do it. I KNEW what I was supposed to do and found every excuse not to. Whatever your calling is WILL keep calling you. Even as I wrote, I found myself slipping into a state of shame, and I questioned so many details like,

"Should I really tell this to the world? Like, it's too much!" How can I expect to walk in freedom if I haven't chosen to walk in forgiveness? This is my authentic story; I should never be embarrassed of anything I've experienced! When we invite God into our lives and into our pain, His healing stabilizes the negative effects of our wounds. His defining of us is more powerful than the negative impact of our life experiences. God builds up our resilience, not only in our daily actions but also in our self-worth.

Being authentic will radiate more pure energy than trying to be an ideal you. I'm thankful for my many dimensions and find comfort in exploring them all. Having to suppress parts of your personality out of the fear of who may be watching is shackling. You're the only person on the planet that gets to be you. It's a simple thought yet so very complex. That's the beauty of you. Spend some time exploring what that really means. Don't be concerned about those who won't understand or relate to your intensity. Whenever you find that you are too much for some people, those are not your people. You will always be too much for someone who doesn't know what they truly want from love or life. Holding to the weight and opinions of others is

> **Being authentic will radiate more pure energy than trying to be an ideal you.**

self-sabotage. When you find yourself, you will then bring your entire existence into a room. You will want to live fully. I want to walk into a room and make it a little better than when I first walked in. You are free to live authentically so when you exit, you know there is nothing left to give.

I think the most beautiful thing about me is my evolution. What I am most proud of is the way I've persevered through my pain. Most importantly, I had to forgive the person I was when I was afraid to step into my potential. I had to forgive the person I was when I was in survival mode. I had to release the opinions and guilt I was carrying. If you want clarity and sustained vision for your purpose, you need to venture into a relationship with God that pushes your boundaries. One in which you are immersed where your feet don't touch the bottom of your comfort zone. It's in this place that you surrender your control and, in exchange, find yourself carried by Him into a purpose that contains the fullness of your authentic life. It is extremely uncomfortable, but I've emerged as a stronger and more powerful woman as a result of this experience.

People will pay you to be exactly who you are. In a job and in your business. When we are lost, it is so easy to get caught up in someone else's movement. We want the success of other people when we don't feel successful ourselves. We see her thriving and living in a reality that we may desire, that we assume what she is doing is what we should be doing, and it's not. Be inspired by others but find your own voice. I don't care how many years it may take; create your own wave. God will not bless who you pretend to be. There are people who are tied to you, need what you have to offer, and are connected to gifts you have that you don't even know you possess. Don't mess around and leave blessings, opportunities, or money on the table trying to be someone else. There's no profit in pretending.

> **Your story will change someone's life.**

At the end of every day, all I want is for the people that come into contact with me to experience a genuine spirit and a pure heart. I want nothing more than for people to see the love of Christ in me because I understand that I may be the only example of His grace that some people see.

Your story will change someone's life. You are an inspiration of what God can do. They will have the courage to believe anything can happen for them once they see you walking in your truth.

Root for Yourself Like You Do for the People Who Don't Even Know You Exist

One of my biggest personal priorities is to grow into the woman I want raising my kids. I want to raise royalty. I am going to. I don't want issues my grandmother or great grandmother had passed down to the next generation. I don't want my children to have to heal from their childhood or have to heal from a broken mom. Many of our battles were inherited. They existed long before we were even born. Although I started doing this work a while ago, this type of work is continuous. And because I recognize it better than anyone else in my family, I know that I am the one anointed to break the cycle. You don't have to live another day of your life feeling that you don't measure up. You don't have to settle for living with the emotional instability that results from insecurities. You don't have to settle for relational chaos, indecisiveness, and unnecessary suffering because of your inaccurate belief systems.

We are the sum of our choices. And as a woman in her thirties, I cannot walk around blaming my circumstances on generational curses. Patterns can be broken. If you don't like something, change it. When you are the first to accomplish something, it will always be the hardest. You can be or do whatever it is that you want, despite your history, but you must raise your standards. It is nobody's job to save another adult. Stop cheering and aweing over someone else's life without checking the queen in your reflection.

It is so much easier to root for someone else because we believe in their ability more than our own. Our greatest fear is ourselves. We are afraid of our own ideas succeeding. Remember that epic idea that you had? An idea so great that it made you a bit overwhelmed from all the possibilities that it could bring? Then you found every reason why it wouldn't succeed.

Ain't nobody going to wear that.
Nobody is going to listen to me.
They won't pay that much for this.
Why would they come to me when they could go anywhere else?

And the list goes on. While it is true that many things can work against your success, the biggest critic, naysayer, and doubter is staring at you in the mirror. You have survived every single thing you thought you wouldn't. So go big, and if it fails, so be it. If you want to feel like you're enough, you must act like it. You must believe it. This does not come for free. You must grow into the emotions you seek. You've spent enough time being scared. All of your self-doubt is scaring the money away. Stop thinking and acting small, you're playing with your own potential.

Stacey,

I forgive you for not recognizing my own power and influence. I forgive you for not trusting your gift and, most importantly, God. I forgive you for seeking validation, approval, and acceptance from anybody other than God. I forgive you for not always understanding your power and not living up to your full potential.

Anastasia

You get to choose what you want, but you must be clear about what you want. This is your number one priority. Decide what you want to be, do, think, and have. Think of your gifts, talents, and abilities. What is it that you do well with ease? What gives you sincere joy? What do you think the most about doing but your fear paralyzes you? Your vision can become your life. You can have whatever you want with no limits. But there's one catch: you MUST feel good about it.

Make Confidence Ooze from Your Pores

You know how you build confidence? Start showing up fully for yourself. What does that look like? Consistency. Consistency bridges the gap from "Who does she think she is?" to *"That's who she is."* Keep doing the things fear says you can't. Keep doing the things laziness will talk you out of. Wake up earlier. Get a daily agenda together. Sometimes we need to see it written down and checked off daily to keep us on track. Look your best. Even if you work from home or don't work directly with others, make a habit of pulling a look together.

There is a quote by Dion Sanders that I live by:

> *"When you look good, you feel good. When you feel good, you do good. And when you do good, you make money."*

It's not always about the money, but the commitment to feeling your best at all times makes you more confident overall. It's a domino effect for you and those around you. Who you are should make others want to discover who they are. When you look and feel your best, the next woman will want to step her game up as well.

> **Trust God's promises even without the details.**

Patience and consistency will get you the greatest results. If you have put something out there, be patient as it is coming together for you. Trust God's promises even without the details. I am just now seeing the physical manifestation of seeds I planted four years ago. Be consistent with your action and faith. The results are coming! When you become what you consistently practice, life will reward you.

The difference between excellence and mediocrity is commitment. So you have to ask yourself, "Am I willing to be all the way in?" Your potential is so valuable and critical that the idea of not fully reaching it should scare you. Thinking about all that I could possibly be leaving on the table alarms me. Did I do everything I possibly could to avoid the demise of mediocrity and settling for a life I know I don't

> **The difference between excellence and mediocrity is commitment.**

want? Someone can have the same cards you were dealt and win. Did I claim the victory with what I was dealt? Or did I throw them down and walk away from the game claiming life is unfair? Or am I too content with my achievements that I am missing the call of God trying to stretch me into new territory? Just because you got used to it or are happy with it doesn't mean it is God's calling for your life. These real questions remove our current layers of complacency and help us see where we truly are in life. Your flesh will talk you out of faith. Your flesh doesn't want you to feel uncomfortable. God will allow you to feel distress for a season that will cause you to become restless. The reason behind this is to get you to seek something beyond where you are!

What is God telling you in life right now? To rest and be still? To change careers? To start a ministry? To be creative? To move to a new city? Walk one step at a time toward God's direction, being careful not to add or take away from what He has told you.

When you are so committed to your personal development, it encourages those around you to grow. It creates a positive ripple effect. Be committed to your personal development because it is a springboard to personal excellence. It's the only way to assure yourself that there's no limit to what you can accomplish. The key to saving the world, your community, and your family is you. You are the key. Heal yourself, know yourself, make yourself whole and free. When you heal yourself, you heal your kids, you heal your parents, you heal your ancestors, you heal your home, you heal your tribe, you heal everyone who sees you healing.

Healing is not the complete disappearance of your pain and trauma. Healing is acknowledging that the pain may still exist but knowing that whatever you've gone through or whatever you're feeling doesn't define you.

Don't Let Your Lack of Confidence Become the Death of Your Calling

How your life feels is more important than how it looks. I'll say that again. How your life FEELS is MORE important than how it LOOKS.

In most cases, we're taught to betray ourselves before anyone else does it to us. It doesn't often look like self-betrayal. It looks like we're simply being nice. As a child, being nice meant stuffing my feelings rather than risk causing friction by expressing them. It meant inviting people to my birthday party that I didn't want to invite to avoid hurting their feelings. It meant being super critical of myself for getting a "C" on that exam instead of an "A" even though I truly tried my best. Sometimes it even meant I had to downplay my talents and passions to spare others the discomfort of envy.

Stacey,

Maybe the journey isn't so much about becoming anything. Maybe it's about un-becoming everything that isn't really you.

Anastasia

Don't get me wrong. There is real wisdom in being considerate of the people around you. Yet if taken too far, we can end up with a fertile seed bed for self-betrayal. As an adult, I had to undo the thought that outer peace is more important than inner peace. If considering others' feelings and excluding our own is the nice thing to do, we learn duty to others trumps duty to ourselves. And if excelling at something makes people envious, we learn it is better to hide our gifts from the world than to outshine others.

The conscious and subconscious messages I received while growing up groomed me to betray myself. Slowly but surely, they became ingrained in my subconscious seemingly without my consent. As a result, I entered adolescence and adulthood believing the needs and feelings of others to be more important than my own.

This belief never served me well. It didn't lead to a happy life. Instead, it led me to betray myself in my relationships. I endured abuse and settled for crumbs instead of getting the whole cake. I didn't get what I deserved. And all the while, I thought it was the right thing to do.

I had to forgive myself for watering myself down. For being afraid of my light. For being so consumed with what others thought about me. For being embarrassed about my own story. For not seeing my own beauty. I had to ask how can I attract abundance if I am afraid to recognize who I am? You can only attract on the level that you are. When you vibrate low, you attract low.

Stacey,

You've paid full price for the person you've become. You better not discount that for nobody.

Anastasia

Self-betrayal can occur within a context of any relationship. Specific exchanges can result in compromising ourselves. Here are a few examples that I've experienced in my personal life:

- Changing myself to be who my partner/friend/family member wants me to be
- Denying problems in my relationships
- Silencing my voice/intuition
- Engaging in undesired intimacy
- Compromising my beliefs
- Sacrificing my values
- Losing my autonomy
- Lying in order to keep the peace

Developing a healthy relationship with our emotions is a roller coaster that will take time, but it's one of the most valuable processes we can experience. Our emotional maturity comes out in how we interact with others and in the way we engage with ourselves.

Here are some signs of emotional maturity that I discovered within myself and others over the past four years:

- Holding space for someone without giving advice (unless asked)
- Setting and keeping boundaries
- Respecting the boundaries of others
- Being honest with myself
- Responding rather than reacting
- Accepting my emotions rather than invalidating or dismissing them
- Taking responsibility and admitting when I am wrong
- Being open, curious, and nonjudgmental toward my own experiences
- Being able to differentiate my feelings from those of others
- Remaining loyal to who I am

I hope you know that you deserve it all. The best, the most honest, the most beautiful, and purest love in the world. Not to be loved by others, but to be loved by yourself. To look in the mirror and think, "Yes, I'm exactly who I want to be." To speak up and be proud of yourself. To be authentic in your every move. To be brave, open, and free. You deserve the nicest and most caring souls to walk into your life. You deserve it all. The entire world.

One day, you will discover that you are fierce, strong, and full of fire. Not even you can stop you because your passion burns brighter than your fears.

FOOLISH FAITH

What if I told you, "You are already everything you are trying to become?"

TRUTH JOURNAL

TRUTH JOURNAL

CHAPTER TEN

WHAT'S THE POINT OF FAITH IF YOU DO NOT BELIEVE GOD CAN PERFORM MIRACLES... FOR YOU?

> "Instead of your shame you will receive a double portion, and instead of your disgrace you will rejoice in your inheritance. And so you will inherit a double portion in your land, and everlasting joy will be yours."
>
> — Isaiah 61:7 New International Version

I SAT AT MY desk, shaking, because today is the BIG day. The day I promised myself that I would take a leap of faith. It's January 20, 2020. I begged and pleaded with God for almost six months that He would give me the clearance to say goodbye to my job and focus on my real estate business and *Foolish Faith*. Initially, I was planning to quit on January 2, the first day we returned from winter break. I decided to change the date because I realized we get three paychecks in January. Ha! I would need all I could get. As I was listening to a sermon on YouTube on this very day, I literally cried at my cubicle. I was almost at the point of hallucination. *Should I? Shouldn't I? What if?* I repeated over and over in my head. I was petrified.

On January 1st, I prayed to God for an expeditious answer.

"God, show me if I can do this, if I am supposed to do this. If not, then put my thoughts and worries to rest."

I had two clients in the works, but no contracts yet. I also had one solid pre-approved buyer who was not under contract yet. But is that enough? What about a few months from now? I really didn't have a lot saved, just a few months' worth. I should get a small tax refund that can hold me, but is this the right move? I don't know the first thing about entrepreneurship. But I knew one thing: that I will not be able to conquer this next level on my own.

"God, I need an answer now more than ever."

On January 2nd, three clients reached out to me. Two reached out about buying in the near future. The third was a past client who was possibly interested in buying a condo. The next day, two more ladies reached out to me via social media. They were not ready to purchase at the moment; one of them was currently going through a first-time buyer program. I began to keep a record of what was happening just so the enemy couldn't confuse me. Sometimes it is necessary to write down what God is doing so your mind doesn't play tricks on you. I was at work, full of anxiety, so I decided to listen to Sarah Jakes Roberts. Anytime I need to get my spirit in order, I plug in my ear buds and turn to her messages on YouTube. The major points on this sermon were:

> "There are people who are anointed, but they don't have the heart for what they are anointed to do. God said He knew you didn't have the heart when he anointed you. But that your obedience is what grows your heart."

She also said...

> "Somebody has committed to some things that are bigger than them that will require more heart than they have the capacity for. But they are taking a step on their anointing. And they are saying that this year will be the year that they take a step on what God has given them. I don't have the heart to do it yet, but I have the obedience, and I am believing that as I activate the obedience, that my Father will expand my heart. That means the business will grow on another level, but you are going to have to do it under pressure."

That statement was everything. That was exactly where I was. And because life had ruffled me up a bit, I was terrified to make yet another bad choice. January 5th was the first Sunday of the year. I vividly remember God speaking to me as I sat in church, urging me to finish *Foolish Faith* in the year 2020. I need to get moving on this now. I believed certain things I wanted Him to do weren't moving because I have not fully walked in what He has asked of me. It was time to stop playing around about the things He has called me to do. I felt a shift coming, and I knew I would need to juggle a lot at one time between what I wanted to do and what God put on my heart to do. What He asks of us will change us more than we ever thought possible. It is never easy; nothing He asks of us is something we can do on our own or apart from Him. It is always something He will ultimately get the glory out of. So I made a promise to myself that I would have *Foolish Faith* finished and edited this year. 2021 will be dedicated to releasing my very first published book.

On January 8th, I told my cousin Danishia everything that was happening, and I was unsure what God was really telling me.

"I don't know if this is God or if my mind is playing tricks on me," I uttered.

"*Why would you think it is not God?*" she asked.

"Because the enemy hears your prayers, too. I don't know, maybe I am just tripping."

"But there is nothing that you could do, right or wrong, that would be out of His control."

As soon as we hung up, I prayed.

"Father God, I thank you for the undiscovered gifts and talents that you have bestowed upon me. I thank you for your unconditional love and never-ending mercy. I confess that I am not consistent in my prayer life and growing my relationship with you as I should, and I ask for your forgiveness. I will no longer use you as a genie, only asking for blessings in a time of crisis. I will remain committed and steadfast to you and your word. I ask that you will give me a direct answer as to how I should move forward in this season. I ask for insight and foresight as I have a desire to release the things you have placed in my heart and my spirit. God, I ask you not just for the favor to carry out the vision, but the wisdom to carry it out well. Father, help me be spiritual in all things but practical as well. This means, Lord, discipline me with my eating, exercise, mental health, and my finances. Let your Holy spirit guide me in every area and facet into my life as this affects how I bring the vision you gave me into fruition. I thank you for the perseverance and drive to see it through. I rebuke defeat, self-sabotage, insecurity, doubt, worry, anxiety, premature plans, premature release, disruption, confusion, stolen ideas, and any other vices that would come *against the vision you gave me. I humbly thank you in advance for all that is to come, and I seal this prayer with thanksgiving and great expectation. In Jesus' Name...*

Amen."

I grew tired of not reaching a goal or feeling a burning desire to do something and holding myself back. Almost making it and giving it a good try no longer satisfied me. I felt that God was in the neighborhood, but for whatever reason, He wouldn't stop at my doorstep. I understood that this next chapter would be difficult, but I needed a definite answer as to if I could quit and be okay. I got out of my car and went into work for another mentally draining day. Literally, twenty minutes later a client said they wanted to sell their condo this month. They were planning to move out of town in May, but things changed. We made an appointment to meet and solidify the contract that next week. I was floored. I couldn't even believe it.

Stacey,

It happened the way it did so I could bring you exactly what you prayed for. Beautiful things are about to happen for you. When you least expect it, God is going to blow your mind.

Anastasia

Over the next week, I would receive inquiries from three additional potential clients. I even spoke to another seller and confirmed I would be able to list their property at the beginning of February. I knew this was the presence of God. I have never seen movement like this in my entire life. My immediate circle was stunned. No one could believe it because up until this point everything—and I mean EVERYTHING—has been so difficult for me to achieve. Like it was poppin'! They knew that God was actively moving in my life. I did too. I took everything gracefully and with care. I believed God told me my overflow season was coming, and I needed to prepare myself. I knew that with all the trouble I was experiencing at my job, I would not be able to manage everything I had coming up because my boss was a jerk. I needed to take the leap and trust in God.

Are You Walking in Faith Even When Your Faith Feels Like It Is Fleeting?

Things would still pan in my favor; a few of the clients I spoke with were not ready in that moment. But I still had a total of four active clients. I was in so much shock. All I wanted to do was to figure out a way to keep God pleased. I'd never experienced this, and I didn't want to mess it up by not holding up my end of the bargain. As much shock as I was in, the enemy went into overdrive to distort the vision I thought was clear. I went from being happy and in disbelief to being fearful. I got scared. The moment you find yourself experiencing happiness, the enemy kicks into overdrive to ruin your plans before you even experience them. The enemy knows God moves on faith, so if he can get you to shift your mindset and walk in fear, you won't be able to witness the miracle you have been praying for. I promised myself I would stand on God's promises this year. I promised myself I wouldn't be a weak, lukewarm Christian. What is the point of going to church if you really don't believe in God? What is the point of quoting Scripture if you aren't going to stand on it? What is the point of tithing if you really don't believe God will take care of your needs?

I needed to prove to myself what I am capable of. I believed that if nothing else, I at least had the courage to try. I was tired of ending year after year in the same place, not feeling proud, and although I wouldn't know how this year would end, *something* would be drastically different. I needed the courage to let go of what I already didn't want in hopes that God would have something better on the other side.

Fast forward to January 20th. I had plans of throwing my boss under the bus for all of the agony he'd put me through. When God began lining up potential clients back to back, I decided that I did not care to make him look bad anymore. I couldn't even believe what God was doing. It was so much greater than anything my former boss had ever done to me. I didn't care if he slandered my name to the ground, there is no greater feeling of God answering a long-awaited prayer. NOTHING. Your enemies cannot bring you off that cloud.

TD Jakes said something very profound in a sermon that always stuck with me:

"You cannot be mighty and petty at the same time."

And the way God has been moving and where I believe He is taking me is not worth me firing shots back at someone I will never have to see again.

I drafted something quickly to turn in for my notice. A one-liner. Just to satisfy HR. The entire day went by. I left it sitting in my email draft because I couldn't find the courage to turn it in. I asked God for another sign. I BEGGED. I PLEADED. He was silent. I followed up with my second seller to make sure we were still set to sign the contract the following weekend. We were still good. I ordered my "For Sale" sign installation. Even with all this, I needed something else. And nothing. I asked God for forgiveness because this was all new to me. I am the first person in my family to take this type of leap of faith. What I was doing was beyond foolish and wouldn't make any sense to anyone, including myself. I felt concerned about disappointing other people. I cared too much about what other people would have to say, and I had to stop living for anyone else's approval. I got up from my desk and took a 20-minute walk. I still didn't come to a resolution. Something like this is difficult because unless they have walked your path NO ONE will understand the pressure you feel on the inside of you to MOVE. I called Danishia to help talk me off the ledge or to push me.

> *"Even though you live in fear of losing your job, your job is the one thing you can control. And even though the money is not enough, it comes in like clockwork, and you can depend on it. Sometimes God calls you to a place where you can only depend on Him to see your miracle. Maybe that is what He wants."*

I went back to my desk, and I hit send on my resignation email.

It was done.

I did it. I couldn't even believe that I did what I did! A place I'd called home for nearly five years, I simply quit.

My boss had already left for the day, so I left a letter on his desk. I couldn't believe it. January 31st would be my last day. I cried again asking God to give me the strength I needed to become the person I had always dreamed of becoming.

I screamed in the car. My entire body was shaking. But as I drove away, I also felt a sense of relief. Have you ever felt great fear and a sigh of relief at the same time?

2020 is the year I will walk on water.

Your Life Unfolds in Proportion to Your Courage

I will be the first to admit, I don't know how to truly be courageous. I come from an ordinary family; being bold is not the norm or the standard that I have been taught. I have been taught to play things safe. Go for what I know. Get my ducks in a row and do what makes sense. But I always felt the tug on my heart for something greater. That there was something else for me that didn't align to what I knew.

It is difficult for most of us to see what we cannot see. Those last two weeks of work, I went from being empowered to feeling weak, to being like, "God, just have your way." I had no clue what I was doing and that was what scared me most. I had many thoughts that questioned if I was truly doing the right thing.

I had no plan whatsoever, and it was the bravest thing I've ever done. I promised myself that in this new decade I would not be dissatisfied in my work or in myself! I am committed to self-discovery, and although I don't know what my purpose is, I plan to unlock new layers of it this year. For the very first time, I am devoted to myself.

What would life be like if we kept our commitments? We tend to use language like "I'm trying" to make ourselves feel better, but when you really want something, no excuse is acceptable. Your self-commitment is you honoring yourself.

When you don't commit to yourself, it will deplete your self-esteem and erode your self-image. Your strength is in your routine. If you're going to get up at 5 a.m., do it. If you're going to exercise after work, do it. If you're going to start a hobby, do it. If you're going to work on your business from 9 p.m. until 11 p.m., do it. I never saw results in anything until I stuck with a routine. Get a routine and stick with it. Nothing happens overnight, but it's the consistency that will yield results. When you complete something on any level, it gives you confidence. Assurance comes from doing. There are many ideas or things I've wanted to do that I did not finish, let alone begin. I spent my years in undergrad pursuing a broadcasting degree. I had all the bomb internships, spent time in NYC for summers working at national networks, and completed several demo reels. Then once it was time to actually land my very first reporting job, I couldn't. I went on several interviews at local stations in small markets, and each time I would make it to the final round only to not be chosen. I remember I sent my reel to be critiqued by a woman I met online who was a top producer at CNN in Atlanta. She watched the entire thing. She made positive remarks about my stories, my writing, even my voice. Her only critique was about how I looked. That I was overweight, and I could stand to lose about 20 lbs. I was truly hurt. I took it to heart, and I believed that to be the reason why I wasn't landing any on-air positions. I wanted to prove her wrong, but the comment stung so badly that I lost the fire I once had to pursue the career. I hate to say it, but after that moment, I pretty much gave up news reporting.

I gave up one of my greatest dreams because of the thoughts and opinions of one individual. Thankfully, even that worked in my favor.

In this age of social media, it is quite common to want to be the first to do something, the youngest to achieve something major, to be the leader in the pack. Please be careful how you place deadlines and timelines on your dreams. Does it come from a place of wanting to challenge and push yourself to reach your goal? Or does it come from a place of fear and impatience? What's for you will never escape you, and what escapes you isn't for you.

You will face adversity in anything you choose to do. People think that if God is in it, everything will align and come together. That is not always the case. The proof of the presence of God is not always comfortable feelings. Sometimes the proof of the presence of God is disruption. Sometimes one thing in your life dies so that something else can come alive. God will cause conflict in order for you to shift and put all of your dependence upon Him. Unless you have received confirmation that the path is not for you, or you truly no longer have a desire for it, do not succumb or become defeated in the process.

When your stories constantly end with you "trying" and not actually "doing," over time you stop believing in yourself. Even more so when you allow the perceptions of others to

> **Remember this: Comfort zones are where dreams go to perish.**

infiltrate your spirit. Don't get me wrong, critique is necessary, but it should only make you fierce, not insecure. Your frustration with yourself will cause you to start developing weak relationships with others. If you can't depend on you or commit to you, how can anyone else? How can you be happy and excited for someone else's accomplishments or success when you are not confident in your ability to complete something?

Your inconsistency is a form of disbelief. Yes, consistency and discipline are hard. The question is: why do you believe you can't do hard things? We don't start because we don't want to seem like a beginner. We don't start because we don't want to be seen "starting from the bottom." We don't start because our "perfectionism" holds us hostage. We don't start because we are so hard on ourselves, and the funny part is, most times no one is ever thinking about you the same way you're thinking about yourself. The noise comes from our own minds. You owe it to yourself and your future to remain focused. I want you to commit to a goal—whether it be through the end of the week or the month, focus on that task and watch how you feel when you complete it!

Remember this: Comfort zones are where dreams go to perish.

FOOLISH FAITH

Sometimes Fear Does Not Subside, and You MUST Do It Afraid

If you wait for the perfect moment, you will wait for the rest of your life. The pressures of your past mistakes and wrong choices may cause you to think you shouldn't pursue a goal, that there isn't enough time, or that you've lost your best years. If you have the courage to believe, your best years are always the years you have left. I made many mistakes and lost a lot in my poor decision making, but God supplied me with more. When God put a calling on your life, He already factored in the foolish decisions you would make. Everything that happens to us was meant to serve us. Even in terrible situations that pain will produce a passion that will heal families, communities, and millions. Therefore, your foolish choices can and still will be factored into the plan for your life. Your circumstances may change you, but they never change your purpose.

What holds most people back isn't the quality of their ideas, but their lack of faith in themselves. This distorted vision of yourself is what's keeping you from the level of life and business that you're so desperately looking for but have yet to step into. Lack of consistency and confidence shows up in how you manage your day, how you lead your family or your team, how you price your services, and even how you take care of yourself. You are the only person you need to convince. You are the only one holding you back. Action is the final step to complete what you're manifesting. Confidence comes by taking action. You have to work to earn your own trust.

Stacey,

You owe it to yourself to try something new, especially if you can't stop thinking about it. Every vision deserves a chance at becoming a reality. What you get by achieving your goals is not as important as who you become by achieving your goals.

Anastasia

As a new entrepreneur, I was extremely nervous about my ability to generate an income outside of a job. I put two new listings on the market that first week, and I was working with one buyer. Even though I am confident in what I provide in my business, the idea that I no longer had a job kept me on my tippiest of toes. I meditated, and no matter what negative thoughts attempted to enter my mind, I forced myself to think positive thoughts. It is fairly easy not to speak what you think, but eliminating thoughts not so much. You can be the most positive person and still experience doubtful thinking. You do, however, have the power to think new thoughts that reflect what you desire to see. When I listed those properties, I did have a moment where I told myself, "What if I can't get it sold?" I didn't allow that thought to live in my mind. Before any fear could creep in, I immediately flipped it to, "I will sell this home quickly with a full price offer and a smooth escrow."

FOOLISH FAITH

Stacey,

You will attract into your life the things you think, feel, and say most often. Anything you need is either within you or within reach.

Anastasia

Our minds are constantly evolving, and they will always require intention and effort on our part no matter where we are in our journey. I still experience doubtful thought patterns, but I have gotten much better in changing the narrative to what I want to manifest, even if I have no idea as to how it is possible. When beginning a new chapter, you will face opposition from yourself in an attempt to force you to believe you aren't ready for what you are praying for.

Following my departure, I told myself I would not be concerned about money, and I didn't expect things to unfold how they did. One of my listings went into escrow that first week and closed in a record 19 days. I actually received a paycheck one month after resigning!

You can LITERALLY speak and manifest blessings into existence.

Don't be surprised at how quickly things get into motion once you have decided. Your faith is what moves God. Anything you do in His name will eventually lead to a positive outcome.

I went from having a client here and there to being in and out of escrows concurrently. I closed deals every single month. What was different from all the prior years to now? I was spiritually weak. I had poor money management habits. I often talked myself out of what I wanted. I lacked self-belief. I lacked confidence. I thought God was upset with me, so I wouldn't receive certain blessings. I wasn't prepared. I couldn't have handled my prayers being answered on this level in previous years. I became comfortable enough with my past to allow it to be just that. I stopped holding myself hostage. It also wasn't my turn. The glory is that much sweeter, and I am more humbled because I had to wait.

At the end of the first quarter, I had sold 1.2M dollars of real estate. I earned 81 percent of my annual income at my old job in my first two months of being self-employed.

Hear me clearly: You can come back from ANYTHING.

Not sure what you are afraid of? Could it possibly be you? Gather courage for yourself. This is a part of life that only you can stand up to. I love the fact that there are certain things in life no one can do for you. You must do it yourself or live with the regret. You have everything you need to save yourself. You are your biggest fight, but you also are your biggest win! Your bag was secured before the ends of the earth were decided on. You're already chasing things that are already yours. Walk in your purpose. Do you really think God would put you in the position to see your dream but not give you the ability to accomplish it?

Align yourself with the things that you know you were called to do. You think it can't be done because you can't get from A to Z today. You make excuses because you don't want to start over again. To go from an unhappy place to a joyful one, you must be brave enough to travel through a scary, vulnerable, lonely place called uncertainty. When you are uncertain, you can't make excuses. It is the opposite of comfort, so it keeps you on top of your game. Until you hate not accomplishing something more than you love complaining about it, you won't make the change.

You can't wait until the fear goes away and then make a move. The fear may not go away. You're going to have to do it in spite of the fear. You're never going to be 100 percent ready, and it's never going to be just the right time, but that's the point. It means that every moment is also the right moment. That's what faith is all about. If you're going to be foolish, be foolish enough to believe that God can do anything.

If You Want to Become HER, It's Time for You to Apply Pressure

I now had ample time to make decisions on how I wanted my life to look and feel. So what was it that I wanted? Asking yourself, "What do I want out of life?" is such a big, open-ended question that will change as you enter and exit various phases. What do I want at this moment? I want to experience peace—which includes going to therapy, reading motivational self-help books, and learning to openly speak about my journey and pitfalls (no matter how embarrassing). I am a HUGE advocate for therapy. I believe in God and am very spiritual, but praying isn't the only answer. Talking to your mama, your significant other, your mentor, your sibling(s), your pastor, your best friend, and that friend that always knows the right thing to say is not a substitute for speaking to a professional therapist. Seeking professional help allowed a lot of things that I didn't realize were suppressed to be exposed. It has allowed me to become okay with being vulnerable and has helped me to mature emotionally and intellectually.

I want to be confident—not fake confident, not social media confident, but confident for real. That meant self-acceptance. I started embracing my flaws. That meant looking at myself in the mirror and saying, "Baby girl, your nose is perfect." Learning to be happy with my physique, to eat like a queen, and to treat my body like the temple that it is. It meant to become secure in that I am a natural observer and often shy around new people. I don't need to be the loudest in the room. My presence is strong enough for the room to adjust to my spirit. Ridding myself of the imposter syndrome. That I can be influenced and look up to those I admire, but what I have to offer is unique to who I am, and that is just as great. To stop comparing. Comparison kills creativity. Nobody can do it with my voice, my experience, or my insight. My gifts are mine for a reason. They may be different from others, but they are just as significant. I am okay with other people being "better" than me. I may not be the smartest, most successful, prettiest woman in the room. Yet I still deserve to be there. I don't need anything other than what I already have. God doesn't judge us based on what He did not give us. I will use and create with the gifts he gave me. My material possessions and accolades are extra. They are wonderful and only enhance who I am, but they do not make nor break who I am.

I want to be authentic—my voice, my thoughts, and my actions are conclusive to who I am at my core. I give myself permission to be free, and I am not obligated to do anything outside of that. I may consider someone else's opinion, but before any decision is made, I consult with myself and ensure that what I engage in reflects truth and honesty in each phase of my life. I no longer abandon myself in an effort to live up to someone's false expectations. I don't abandon my truth. I walk in full transparency. I don't pretend to be someone I am not. I own my truth in such a way that no one can use it against me. Stepping into my authenticity gave me the authority to know that God loves me regardless of where I come from and what my circumstances look like. I know that I am a work in progress, and the finished product will be absolutely worth it.

I want to be fulfilled—I only make moves when my heart is in it, and my work is true to who I am. My positive affirmations create new avenues of abundance in my life. I let down my guard and do what feels natural because those who matter don't mind, and those who mind don't matter. I don't have pity parties over what doesn't work out. Every closed door puts me on the road to something greater. I bring my WHOLE entire self to every situation, including business, where it is most critical. I know and have accepted that I cannot control what anyone thinks of me, and I am secure in the fact that I will attract the right people and situations in my life. Authenticity matters. By being honest and authentic, my clients and colleagues trust me. By being myself, I empower other women, and men, around me to do the same.

Stacey,

Allowing yourself to be imperfect was one of the kindest things you have ever done. It didn't just change your life. It changed your aura, which changed everyone in your life.

Anastasia

When God restores things and people in our lives, we have this misconception that He will bring it back to its "original" state. But oftentimes when God restores, He does away with the old and replaces it with something better—better thoughts, better people, better circumstances. Although not knowing what that better is makes us uncomfortable.

Confidence is *not* comfortable. Yup, read that again, babe.

Confidence is anything but comfort. It's showing up, taking up space, overcoming yourself, your doubt, your fear, and your negative self-talk. Choosing confidence means facing hard emotions. Choosing confidence over comfort takes practice. Stop moving as if you will be small forever! You feel stuck because you have yet to see how big of a deal you are. You don't realize the level of impact you can have on the world. The journey to becoming confident is hard, and you will have difficult moments, but it's the only way you can truly become masterful at the practice. Your suffering can produce something of great value, and I've gained a new appreciation for the difficulties of life. I am more committed than ever to living each day with passion and purpose.

This is the gold that God has produced in my life. He can do the same in your life when you allow him to use your pain and your story for his glory. Your beliefs about your abilities will manifest, so be careful what you say you can't do.

Maybe I Don't Want to Be Someone Else's Woman. Maybe I Want to Be My Own Woman.

Following my divorce, I decided to fully commit myself to healing and self-love. I was heartbroken and upset by what I'd settled for and tolerated. It took me a very long time to accept and move past never receiving an apology, but it forced me to create boundaries. My level of self-preservation is at an all-time high. I no longer want to concern myself with searching for love from another person without first fully exploring the depths of my own love.

Stacey,

It's not because God wants to see if you can do it on your own. He already knows you can. He desperately needs YOU to see you can do it all alone. To stand strong in your power, stand strong in your worth. You, my dear, are chosen.

Anastasia

I made the choice to abstain from sex. Celibacy is the greatest decision I have ever made. I am not miserable (I don't know why people thought I would be). I don't regret it. I have developed immense self-control. It has made me strong. It changed my perception of what I thought I needed to be happy. Most of all, it has brought me closer to God. It has also allowed me to achieve quite a few of my goals. You think I could've accomplished publishing this book, launching a YouTube channel, beginning an office stationery line, obtaining an MBA, quitting my job of nearly five years, growing Anastasia's Luxury Living full time, purchasing my first investment property, getting back into the 700+ credit club, increasing my savings account to six figures, finally conquering my frequent yo-yo dieting issues, and loving myself like never before with a narcissistic man by my side? Ehhh...it's possible. But this just hits differently. I was able to have laser sharp focus and not be distracted by a relationship or situation that would not benefit my goals or my mental health in the long run.

Stacey,

When God says He will give you back better than what you've lost...believe Him.

Anastasia

I thought I would need someone to help me in reaching my goals. That I *needed* a husband. In this season, God showed me that much of where I thought I needed the help of a man, I was able to do alone. God will put you by yourself because He needs YOU to realize you don't need anyone else but Him. I believe men and women need each other, but not as a crutch or co-dependency. I still desire to be married again in the future; however, the purpose of why I want it is different. I want my children to witness a strong family structure. I want to break generational curses with my husband. I want us to take one another's purpose and help expand it beyond what we could do on our own. Being celibate allowed me to discover myself, and I realized that it actually feels good to be stingy with my body. Removing sex and money from the table shows you that many individuals have nothing outside of that to offer.

Not engaging in sexual activities boosted my confidence and self-esteem like never before. I no longer succumb to lust or my own emotions. I am fully and completely in control of my emotions. I am whole. I began to recognize what I am worthy of. I believe every woman should experience a season of celibacy. It doesn't have to be as long as I did, and I know a few of you may be rolling your eyes, but this time could be the reboot you're looking for in more ways than one. In a world that seems obsessed with love, sex, and relationships, remaining single on purpose is a big statement. It's an empowering thing to say "no" to your own body and stick to it for any moment in time. It's a gift you are giving to yourself. When you make repeat choices that are detrimental to yourself and your well-being, you have to take a step back and examine what is disrupted within you. Many women experience losing themselves and their identities in the pursuit of men. Sex with multiple partners brings about soul ties, unhealthy connections, drama, unstable hormones, a jacked-up pH balance, and heartbreak. When I cut out all of the noise that I was creating around myself with unhealthy people and decisions, I was able to become more in tune with who I was and who I had *forgotten* I was. Even a single year of celibacy could be just the thing to snap you out of that pattern and help you regain connection to your own identity.

In 2020, after four years of being celibate, I opened my heart to dating. In the midst of developing new connections with men, *I knew who I was again.* **I liked who I was again.** I can tell the difference in the caliber of men I attract. I operate in divine femininity, and I understand how powerful it is. A woman's self-esteem is reflected in the type of man she attracts and ultimately chooses. Ladies, you have no idea how your very essence can change a man's life. When you combine your intellect, wit, charm, relatability, beauty, sophistication, poise, and gentleness, you have one hell of a potion. We were created to be like magic; however, life's trials have caused us to diminish ourselves. In order for us to reclaim our aura, we must know and move how we were created to be.

Stacey,

It took you decades to truly fall in love with yourself. I am so glad you found your way home. Perfect timing.

Anastasia

When I do finally allow myself to be chosen, it will be because our values and standards align. There must be a divine energy that connects us. I am ready to be a healthy partner for someone. I don't apologize for not meeting someone on their level. Their frequency must match my own.

> **High standards protect you from low quality experiences.**

High standards protect you from low quality experiences.

Someone I loved once gave me a box full of darkness. I now understand that too was a gift. Thank you to the individuals who didn't want what I had. Those experiences changed and ushered me into a new dimension. This lane requires being properly courted and requires a man to earn his way into my heart—a man who is ready to receive what I have to offer.

How did I keep the faith that there would be someone better? I was that someone better. I became comfortable being alone. I did not believe singleness was a punishment. I knew that evolving into my highest self would attract better quality men - and it did.

Nothing good ever comes to a woman who settles.

Somebody Is Watching You and Learning How to Trust God. Your Example Matters.

When coronavirus overtook our lives in 2020 and stay-at-home orders were put into place, just like many of you, I had concerns of how this pandemic would impact my life and my future. In the blink of an eye, we went from planning to experience what was looking like our best year yet to being laid off, having to close our businesses, family and friends contracting COVID-19, cancelling vacations, postponing graduations and weddings, and being forced to physically distance ourselves from our loved ones. Headed into the final quarter of 2020, this is our normal. We are still unsure about how our lives will look in the next three months and beyond. For those of us who have made it to see the end of 2020, we are immensely grateful and blessed. If our closest loved ones got to see it with us, we are *even more blessed.*

If nothing else, the time we were forced to spend sitting allowed us to rethink what is truly important. We have spent more quality time with family than we have in a very long time, found or discovered new hobbies, and we even completed projects that have been put off for months if not years. While we all know what went wrong with this year, and we crack jokes about flying back to 2019 or even never speaking of 2020 again, there have been a few upsides as well.

Anastasia's Luxury Living was blossoming. I have a brand and a business that people have begun to recognize. My days are filled with new client consultations, on-boarding new clients, and home shopping with newly pre-approved buyers. I took on my biggest listing to date—literally the day the stay-at-home orders were enacted—and I could not get it sold. It was a luxury home, and in this particular neighborhood, they are on market an average of 60 days. I completed a full marketing plan, beautiful photos and video, brochures, mailings, email blasts, social media—I was totally ready to kill it and add #LuxuryRealtor in my bio and...nothing.

Before I take on a new client, prior to viewing homes—even prior to placing offers—I pray for my clients, their best interests, and that I am the perfect woman to get the job done. I knew coronavirus had put a pause on the real estate market, but in true Anastasia nature, I blamed myself. I did everything I learned through various classes, tips from my mentors—even the price was slightly lower than our comparables. My sellers were extremely nice and understanding of what was going on. However, I began feeling as though I wasn't good enough. Maybe I needed to stay within certain price points. Maybe I wasn't cut out for the luxury market. After two and a half months on the market, my clients wanted to cancel the listing. They started a home-based business producing face masks that took off and needed the space as they were preparing to hire assistants. They were planning to downsize and were ecstatic things happened exactly as they did. I was happy simply because they were happy. Sometimes the blessing isn't always for you but for you to witness what He can do for someone else.

I still felt uncertain, however. The spring market was moving very slowly. I had clients who were afraid of our uncertain market, put a hold on their buying or selling process, or ultimately backed out of deals altogether. I lost about $44,000 in contracts in the spring months. Where I was once confi-

> **If your faith can't be tested, it can't be trusted.**

dent and assured, I began to question if God was still with me. From what happened in January to what was happening now, it felt like He turned His face. I thought I had done something wrong. My biggest fear was going back to the place where I believed God was angry with me. I tried my hardest to do everything right; I paid my tithes on every check I received, I helped others, and my heart was still in a humble place because when you finally come out of something you are just so grateful.

When we're in fear, we don't trust that there is more available to us. We begin to make ourselves small. We shift our energy, and we focus on and create more of the very thing we want to avoid—which is lack.

When there is doubt in your power, there is doubt in God's ability. And so, when you do not trust in yourself, you ultimately do not trust in God.

If your faith can't be tested, it can't be trusted. God proves his presence by putting you in impossible situations. Some of us are better at surviving in famine than we are at thriving in a blessing. I had to rid myself of the subconscious programming that nothing in life comes easy. Everything I want and need flows to me easily and abundantly. In order for good things to come your way, you need to believe you deserve them.

About a month before my 33rd birthday, I bought a new journal. I wrote Hebrews 4:16 at the top of the first page:

Come boldly to the throne of grace, that we may obtain mercy and find grace to help in time of need.

August 13, 2020
My final quarter of 2020 will be better than the entire year! Those contracts I lost were what I needed to reach my goal. Although I am discouraged, I won't live here. I will now double the $44,000 I lost to $88,000. I am not sure how I will make this happen, or if it is even possible. My job is not to worry about the how. I simply need to keep my focus and do the work. A lot of things have transpired this year but this isn't the time to shrink or hold myself back. My gifts and talents are making room for me. I am committed to taking up space. I will stop acting like I am afraid of my own power and start moving as my highest self, completely and unapologetically.

I moved like it was already done. I dressed and showed up like I was selling million-dollar homes. I already created an amazing experience for each client, but I stepped it up and made sure they felt like they were luxury clientele. I remembered what God had done in January. When we are between seasons, we often need to remind ourselves of the things God has done for us previously. Not for His sake, but because WE forget. We forget His promises. We often fail to remember how God has carried us through time and time again.

A few weeks passed before I saw a shift. I continuously declared what I wrote in my journal. I showed up every single day like it came to pass. Suddenly (I love that word), the shift happened right in time for my birthday. My two clients went to five, and one escrow went to three. Each month was increasing subsequently better than the last. The market was on fire, and I effortlessly got buyers into escrow and to the closing table with ease. It was day and night. Was this for real?

Stacey,

You are what you were searching for all along. You were never called to be like them. God did a brand-new thing in and through you. The child in you is so proud of who you have become. I love you.

Anastasia

God uses people who fortify their faith. He allows long periods of silence and isolation to build character and endurance. He doesn't always give warning when that season is up. One day, you will look up, and things will start falling into place like never before.

By Christmas, everything I wrote came to fruition. I was bolder. I took up all the space. I showed up for myself and my business in a way that I wasn't sure I had inside of me. I began filming content for my business and *Foolish Faith*. I made plans and preparations for all that God has put on my heart, and I didn't let anyone else or *myself* stop me. I created multiple streams of income for myself, and I feel more fulfilled than I ever have. I completed the tasks that God gave me. It wasn't that I wasn't afraid, but my passion for greater burned brighter than my fears. Sometimes you have to become a different version of yourself before your vision can manifest. Oh yeah, those cancelled contracts I mentioned? I doubled those numbers. By the end of 2020, I went on to triple my income from the previous year. How many times have I limited what I could receive because of who I thought I wasn't? I have gained every single thing I lost, plus some extra blessings I didn't even qualify for. The confidence I have is not because of what I did, but because every time I think I should doubt God, He shows me that He's never, ever forgotten about me nor given up on me.

You can regret a decision and STILL end up in the right place. You can feel like you've wasted years and still make up for lost time. Everything can happen for your good... EVERYTHING. You create truth and reality with your tongue and thoughts. Be protective over this mega power God gave you, and remove yourself from anyone who influences you to speak or think anything other than the energy and reality you wish to build in your life.

Stacey,

What if the time you thought you lost was the time God needed to prepare the world to receive your gift?

Anastasia

You can't run from your calling anymore. You can't avoid the transformation anymore. This upcoming year is about YOU. It is about your voice and your power. You may be afraid, but you must move within the fear. Your wings already exist; you are the person you've been waiting for. It is critical to the survival of your faith that you stop believing the lie. You are worthy of anything your mind can conceive. I don't care how many mistakes you made, or how many people have said you would never get over that hurdle; your past self is not your current identity. You still deserve it all. You can still have that dream. You can still think new thoughts. You can still create a bomb life. Who you were does NOT disqualify you. We don't pray because of who we are—we pray because of who God is. You were worthy before, and you are just as worthy now. You have already given God a million reasons not to love you. None of them have changed His mind. This is what *Foolish Faith* is all about. God is waiting on you to step into your purpose and pay you back tenfold for everything that you've been though. When your moment arrives, every single experience will make sense.

Stacey,

In search of self, you found truth. In search of truth, you found love. In search of love, you found God. And in God, you found everything.

Anastasia

Had I never been so emotionally shattered, had I not been insecure, had I not made the wrong choices, had it not been difficult, had I not been all cried out, had I not abandoned God, had I not waited for years, had I gotten what I thought I wanted, I would have never shifted and elevated into the space that I am in today. Though I was certain I was being punished, I didn't see the importance of my unique process. But it is now flowing together better than I could imagine. It is important to remember that as beautiful as roses are, they come with thorns. It was all worth the journey to get to this place of unwavering peace I am experiencing now. I am living life on my own terms. I am in full bloom.

Yes, you believe in God. But do you BELIEVE GOD?

TRUTH JOURNAL

TRUTH JOURNAL

Happy 33rd Birthday, Stacey!

Woman, you are fierce and fearless! What a joy it is to witness you blossom into your most authentic, confident self. The version of yourself that you used to dream of, you saw glimpses of her, but you couldn't quite reach out and touch her. Remember her? She's here.

You are not what has happened to you, but what you chose to become. It took immense courage to leave the past behind and take that first step forward. But in doing so, you found the way out of the dark times and into the light of new and better ones.

Girlllllll...you even quit your job! Lord knows you hated that place, LOL. You are doing what you are called to do. Don't ever be afraid to be the full package. You make the rules about who you are and what you do. Your happiness is deserved. You are doing YOU in your own unique way. You do not shrink yourself to fit in places you've outgrown, and settling for less than your worth is not something you can comprehend any longer. Don't ever be afraid to continuously step out on faith. How else will you see the mountains move? Be so bold, so confident in your endeavors, that people stop questioning you and start questioning themselves.

Not everyone will understand, approve, applaud, affirm, celebrate, support, stay, or encourage you in this new season of courageousness. Everything that's great in your life came from doing what was in your heart, not what was expected of you. You define your truth. You define yourself. You are the creator of your story.

Even when your circumstances convinced you that you were no longer deserving of a dream life, God stepped in and showed you that your scars may have changed you, but the way He loves you hasn't wavered. You are even MORE worthy of your heart's desires. You don't deserve His grace, but He gave it to you anyway.

Who would have thought this force of a woman would rise after a divorce? In that time of rock-bottom, you made friends with your grief and insecurities in ways you've never done before. For the first time, you acknowledged your inner child, faced your own darkness, owned your part, and saw the ways you hadn't shown up as a present, confident, and healthy version of yourself. You saw the marriage for what it was—two hurt people playing out their old traumas. It may have crumbled in a fury of lies, betrayal, and deception with you losing "everything," but you were able to meet your wounds in a profound space of solitude. As painful as it was, your divorce was the greatest gift in your life thus far. However, I am most proud that you have rid yourself of the shame you carried.

You graced the fire and yet never smelled like smoke. You've risen from the ashes and returned home to your purest self. You are whole without someone else. You are a complete masterpiece all by yourself, and you do not need a partner to validate your existence. You deserve a love that is unwavering, and first, you gave that gift to yourself.

This season actually WAS about you losing yourself. It was about searching rather than having an answer. You didn't fail; you needed to see the world from a different lens, a different place, and a humble ground. It wasn't as easy as saying you had your heart broken. You needed to have more time for yourself and learn to know what it was like to fall in love with your own warmth, happiness, kindness, and confidence again. Struggle was not your enemy. It was the opportunity to learn to accept and redefine who you are, what you've done, and who you are learning to become.

You've learned the power of impossible situations. If God is only giving you what you CAN handle, you're not learning to depend on Him. Nor are you stepping out in faith. In fact, when you're facing situations that are far beyond your control, God is trusting you more than you trust Him.

God showed you that prayer truly does work. Your prayers never fell on deaf ears. When God listened to your voicemails, He answered them all at once. You have witnessed how God moves when your faith doesn't waiver even when you can't see the path in front of you. You stood in faith, during the hardest time in your life. You believe in the unexpected...a sudden shift...an out of the blue miracle...a possibility of an instant breakthrough. You loosened up about how things will happen. You became open and receptive to abundance and what life has to offer. You raised your vibration, and you exude sophistication and excellence. Everything you once wanted you are now attracting into your life. The thing about God is that He will recover for you in an instant what you've spent years trying to attain. At 33, you have learned the beauty of God's divine timing.

    Stacey, you have transformed every aspect of your life. The little girl you once were is so proud of the woman you are today.

    You are beautiful. You are worthy. You are enough.

    You are built to handle the pressure that comes with your calling. Continue to stand in your power.

I love the woman you've become,
Anastasia

FINAL THOUGHTS

What if your storm was sent so God could prove His presence?

Your life message includes your testimony and your trials. There is a flame that is connected to your purpose. It will set everything ablaze the moment you step into it. You are going to change the world with what God put inside of you. Your miracle is not for your personal enjoyment, but for God's will to be done. God will take the "who" that you are, add Himself, and change everything in your entire life. Don't allow what you know about yourself to become a distraction in getting to your purpose. How can we experience the glory that comes from sharing our testimonies if we refuse to share our story? The world needs to hear your message and what you've overcome. Wear your journey as a badge of honor.

ACKNOWLEDGMENTS

Foolish Faith would not have been possible without the divine plan of God. I am so incredibly thankful for His endless grace and mercy. Thank you, God, for chance after chance to get things right.

I am nothing without my mother and father, Ethel Davenport and Kent Hunter. The values they've instilled in me, unconditional love, and support is the reason I have blossomed into the woman I am today.

Mommy, in the midst of my divorce, you made the choice to find a new job and move your entire life from Wisconsin to California to be with me. You gave up your comfort, everything that you knew and built, and I do not take that for granted. I don't know how I can repay you. I pray one day I will truly be able to make you proud.

My cousin Danishia, you have been with me through some of my craziest moments. Truth is, I never had it in me to become an author until you told me that I needed to write this. Thank you for being my no-judgment vault of secrets.

Aunt Teri, the one who keeps me accountable. Who would have thought six months after you purchased your own home with me you would need to provide me with one? Whew. You have my whole heart.

Lova, you were the first person to read *Foolish Faith*. Thank you for reading, editing, and your endless support.

To all of my family and friends who prayed for, encouraged, and supported me—at any phase of this journey, I thank you. There have been many times I have felt defeated. Thank you for lifting me higher when I didn't have the strength. I am so appreciative that you have been a part of this experience with me. I love you all.

www.ingramcontent.com/pod-product-compliance
Lightning Source LLC
Chambersburg PA
CBHW071428070526
44578CB00001B/38